BEYOND THE OBVIOUS

BEYOND THE OBVIOUS

KILLER QUESTIONS THAT SPARK
GAME-CHANGING INNOVATION

PHIL MCKINNEY

Ⓗ Ⓨ Ⓟ Ⓔ Ⓡ Ⓘ Ⓞ Ⓝ

New York

Library of Congress Cataloging-in-Publication Data

McKinney, Phil.
   Beyond the obvious : killer questions that spark game-changing innovation / Phil McKinney.—1st ed.
       p. cm.
   Includes bibliographical references and index.
   ISBN 978-1-4013-2446-9
 1. Creative thinking.   2. Creative ability in business.   3. Technological innovations.   4. Diffusion of innovations.   I. Title.
   HD53.M39 2012
   658.4'063—dc23
           2011041828

Hyperion books are available for special promotions and premiums. For details contact the HarperCollins Special Markets Department in the New York office at 212-207-7528, fax 212-207-7222, or email spsales@harpercollins.com.

Book design by Renato Stanisic

FIRST EDITION

10   9   8   7   6   5   4   3   2   1

SUSTAINABLE FORESTRY INITIATIVE   Certified Fiber Sourcing   www.sfiprogram.org

THIS LABEL APPLIES TO TEXT STOCK

We try to produce the most beautiful books possible, and we are also extremely concerned about the impact of our manufacturing process on the forests of the world and the environment as a whole. Accordingly, we've made sure that all of the paper we use has been certified as coming from forests that are managed, to ensure the protection of the people and wildlife dependent upon them.

*To my parents, Bill and Arlene McKinney,
for teaching me the rule of success: "Any job worth doing is worth
doing right." I wish you were here to see this.*

Contents

Preface

Today's business world is a rapidly changing place, and new rules for success in it are quickly emerging. First and foremost among them, though, is this: Ideas are your most valuable currency, and your success will be determined by your ability to generate ones that lead to innovations your customers want. In *Beyond the Obvious*, my goal is to teach you how to live by that rule so that no breakthrough idea goes unexplored. Competition is fierce, and there's simply no room for missed opportunities anymore.

Never has this been more apparent than now, as I write this preface. The last few months have been interesting times, to say the least, at HP. In August, HP's Board of Directors announced a significant change in strategy that included (1) shutting down the webOS (formerly Palm) phone and tablet business and (2) looking into spinning off the $40 billion PC (Personal Systems Group) division. In the midst of these changes in strategy, I made the decision to retire from HP after nine years of leading the innovation team.

The timing is interesting because these changes happened months after the final draft of *Beyond the Obvious* was submitted and accepted by my publisher. However, as I re-read the manuscript in the context of these changes, the lessons of *Beyond the Obvious* hold as true as ever. This is a book about generating breakthrough innovations, and that's exactly what my team at HP did. The book is *also* about negotiating both the forces inside your organization that challenge innovation efforts (e.g., obstructionist colleagues I call "corporate antibodies") and the curve balls that come from outside it (e.g., shifts in the global economy or consumer spending). The suggestions I share in this book come from the experience I've gained in these very trenches myself. In the end, my experience is not that different from yours; we are all dealing with companies and industries in a state of flux and uncertainty.

No organization gets it 100 percent right. Innovation is a balance between multiple factors and priorities, as anyone who has ever taken a risk with a new idea knows.

That said, these fundamental shifts in strategy have tremendous potential for productive change. In fact, I call them "jolts" because, like earthquakes, they are unpredictable, seismic events that strike a business or industry without notice, completely altering a once-familiar landscape. I've experienced "jolts" several times in my career, and they've always felt the same: unsettling at first, and then invigorating, as they shake open opportunities for radical change, both on a personal and corporate level. Whatever happens, I know one thing: The spirit of innovation abhors a vacuum, and human ingenuity wants to flourish in all organizations. My goal in this book is to give you the skills you need to find it, foster it, and harness its power in yours.

Phil McKinney
November 2011

BEYOND THE OBVIOUS

Beyond the Obvious

n my career in the technology field, I'm surrounded by visual clues that clearly indicate when a tech product is headed to the gadget graveyard. Most of the time, it's hard to ignore these clues, because they are pretty obvious. I see them in meetings with my coworkers or customers when we take our places in a conference room and pull out our smart phones, tablets, and PCs. In fact, when people have two-year-old laptops in Silicon Valley, they can be pretty sheepish about it. After all, the technology industry is built on the idea of the "refresh"—the tech term for the process of upgrading existing products to keep them feeling new and relevant. The refresh cycle is what makes someone with a perfectly functioning smart phone start to feel anxious when he hears rumors of an upgraded new version about to be released. Even if he doesn't need the improved speed or capacity, he doesn't want to be the person using last year's phone in front of his competitors or clients.

You can make an argument about whether the refresh culture is good or bad, but that's a different book. The point here is that I'm able to see the constant progression of innovation and obsolescence in the life cycles of my products played out in front of my eyes. I don't have to wonder if the Palm Treo is still up to date; the fact that I haven't seen one pulled out in the last few years tells me all I need to know. It's the same feeling that a homeowner gets when he looks at the avocado bathroom he installed in the mid-'70s. You don't need to ask if it's out-of-date; it clearly is.

But as I looked at these outdated gadgets, I realized that they were a perfect metaphor for one of the most important questions that businesses aren't asking, but should be: How do you know when the core beliefs of your business—those about what you do, how you do it, and for whom—have gone from innovative to obvious and are heading toward obsolescence? These beliefs don't come with clunky features, and they don't suffer from inelegant design—at least, not that you can readily see. What are the signs that might tell you that you are reaching a critical moment where you need to dramatically change what you do to avoid getting beaten by your competitors? How do you apply the "refresh" concept to your business to create the kind of continuous reinvention it so badly needs to survive?

All ideas, products, and concepts have a natural progression; you can at least retrospectively follow their evolution from one generation to the next. Look back at the succession of laptops and phones you've owned throughout your life. There's probably a pretty obvious timeline in terms of both their physical characteristics and their technical abilities. However, it's not always easy to recognize the need to evolve or know how to lead this evolution within your organization. It's critical, though, to understand that the supercharged pace of change and innovation means that what was true yesterday is already on its way to being outmoded today. The real winners in the marketplace are those who can get *beyond the obvious* ideas about what their product is, who it is for, and how it is created; break away from the pack; and do something different. If you don't, your competitors will—and you will be left behind.

I picked the title *Beyond the Obvious* because it is simple, straightforward, and cuts to the heart of a problem that many businesspeople, entrepreneurs, and would-be innovators suffer from. Simply put, we are all shaped by our past experiences, whether good or bad. We look at the end results of these experiences—"this idea worked"; "this idea failed"—and consciously or unconsciously turn these results into the rules by which we operate in the present. Sometimes these rules, or assumptions, are smart and valuable. However, the problems begin when we forget that these rules are a snapshot of an old paradigm or set of circumstances. In many cases, the world has moved on, but we are still clinging to the "obvious" ideas that were once true in the rapidly receding past. In order to progress, we need to learn to identify and ignore these "obvious" rules, ideas, or beliefs, and make room for the current conditions our companies operate in.

WHAT THIS BOOK WILL DO

The goal of *Beyond the Obvious* is twofold. First, I want to help you to reevaluate the "obvious," or those old beliefs you learned in your past. These old beliefs are often so integral to your way of doing things that you are completely unaware you even have them. Yet they are setting the parameters for what you do, how you do it, and who you do it for. The only way to break free of them is to identify and analyze them to see if they still hold true. The second goal of *Beyond the Obvious* is to give you a structured and logical system of innovation, one that helps you identify the truly radical and valuable ideas and ignore the others.

Innovation isn't easy; it takes a lot of work and effort to come up with a radical new idea. This is actually a *good* thing. It means that the ability to innovate is a universal skill rather than an act of serendipity, and furthermore rather than luck, the most important thing you need to become an innovator is an organized and methodical way to generate, prioritize, and execute great ideas. My system is called the Killer Questions, and using it will give you a road map to do this. By asking the Killer Questions, you'll be able to create killer ideas with confidence and have faith that you've made the best decision about which ideas to throw your money, time, and effort into developing.

To help illustrate this process, throughout the course of *Beyond the Obvious* we'll be looking at those organizations that realized that they needed to let go of their assumptions and re-ask the core questions about themselves and their industry: "Who are we? Who is our customer? What do we do? Why do we do it this way?" For example, remember when Ma Bell (also known as pre-divestiture AT&T) was split into the "Baby Bells"? One of the babies was Southwestern Bell (SBC), which served states such as Arkansas, Kansas, Missouri, Texas, and parts of Oklahoma.[1] Now, what are the limitations of these areas? For the most part, you're looking at a fixed and relatively small rural population. Sure, there is no competition, so you're not going to be losing business, but you won't be gaining much either. The management team at SBC, and probably at all the Baby Bells, felt they had a safe and comfortable status quo. Business conditions might not radically improve, but they weren't going to drastically decline, either. Fast-forward to 1996, when the Telecom Act opened up the phone lines to anyone who wanted to start their own telecom business.[2] These "anyones" included me. I joined a start-up called Teligent that was formed to compete against the Baby Bells. It was a perfect business opportunity. We were going after a comfortable, safe monopoly that had a tradition of doing business in a certain way. We knew that with some ingenuity and hard work we could run circles around them, and offer their customers new services that the old guys had never considered before. Up until that moment, the telecom companies could rely on one obvious fact: They had access to phone lines; very few other people did. The Telecom Act changed that overnight and was a classic *Beyond the Obvious* moment. All the rules and assumptions were out the window.

Back in Texas, the management team at SBC was looking nervously at companies like Teligent.[3] Suddenly, the safe and comfortable status quo didn't seem like such a stable situation after all. Since there was a limited pool of potential new customers, they realized that they had to give their customers a reason to stay with them rather than switch their business to a flashy new start-up. They realized that they might not be able to compete on price, but they could compete on convenience by bundling together services. They began offering a "Triple

Play," in which customers could get their landline, cable, and mobile all on one bill. SBC then began acquiring other Baby Bells such as Ameritech and Bell South.[4] Recently, they acquired AT&T and, in a neat circularity, they've pretty much returned to where they started from and are now known as AT&T themselves.[5] SBC got out ahead because they recognized that the old way of doing things was obsolete and that they needed to come up with a new way. I can safely make one assumption about the meetings where this new strategy was hashed out: Somebody was asking tough questions and refusing to accept that the rules about how they did business still applied to the post-1996 world.

RECOGNIZING THE OBVIOUS

Sometimes the clues that a business or organization needs to change are subtler than in the example above. You may not have a federally mandated change in your industry to contend with. It could be something closer to home, something that has long ago defaulted to the "obviously" correct way to operate. In this kind of situation, you can't simply count on your own insight to recognize that you are relying on an old answer. You need tools to ask, "What is the *obvious*?"

Sometimes it can take extreme situations to push us past our natural tendency to stick with the "what works." However, we all possess the ability to rapidly innovate when we are threatened with a serious situation; the trick is to learn how to access that energy and focus to create a continuous funnel of innovations.

Think of the NASA engineers who had to improvise a filter to clear the air of potentially lethal carbon monoxide on board Apollo 13.[6] They used a piece of towel, duct tape, and other random items that were aboard the spacecraft; and it worked. I'm guessing they were both terrified at the thought of failing and exhilarated as their Rube Goldberg patch came together. And when all was done, they probably felt the most intense elation of their lives because they'd cobbled together a miracle against all the odds.

Of course, *Beyond the Obvious* is not simply a book about other people's successes. Instead, it is a learning device to help you to unleash your own ability to innovate just as the executives at SBC or the engineers at NASA did. Maybe you think you've got this covered and you're not the kind of person who automatically jumps to the obvious solutions when faced with a challenge. It is possible, though, that you are using answers that have served you in the past and that you believe will continue to serve you in the future.

For example, what do you think of when you read the following?:

Mary had a little ___.
These boots are made for ___.
Happy birthday to ___.

I'm guessing that as you read them you filled in the missing words: "lamb," "walking," and "you." Nature abhors a vacuum—and so does your mind—so your automatic reaction is to fill in the blank. In this situation, the answers are obvious, right?

Our need to "fill in the blanks" and create order and organization is one of the building blocks of cooperative civilizations. But this same instinct is a problem if you are looking to come up with a creative idea or product, especially if you and your competitors are seeking answers for the same problem. If everyone is instinctively and unconsciously jumping to the instant and obvious idea that Mary still likes lambs, it doesn't leave much room to explore whether she'd prefer a Ferrari if offered the option.

Those of us who went through a traditional educational experience are doing exactly what we were taught to do by answering quickly with the obvious solutions. If you were able to push beyond the obvious response and fill in missing words other than "lamb," "walking," and "you," that's a great start. In all likelihood, though, you stopped thinking once you had an answer—in the same way that you stop looking for your car keys once you've found them. You found what you needed, case closed, on to the next.

So, if you gave the obvious "correct" answers, you're not alone. Every year, I selected summer interns for jobs at HP. Now, there was nothing wrong with the minds of the young men and women who competed to land a coveted position on the innovation team at HP. We knew they were the smartest and the brightest. After all, they came with impressive certificates, test scores, and letters of recommendation from their professors to prove it. Want to know the π percent of 1,337? No problem. Don't even need a calculator, it's 42. Curious to know the development process that went into Deutsch-Jozsa algorithm? Check. The problem is, I rarely wanted answers to either of those questions. What I was really looking for was a spark, a fearless sense of inquiry, creativity, and critical-thinking skills. An intellectual precociousness. Audacity. A belief that they—perhaps still teenagers—had the right to question assumptions and to look at the problem or opportunity in ways I hadn't considered. And you wouldn't believe how few of our supereducated minds possessed this ability. Most simply saw the objective as being how fast they could arrive at the answer to my question, just as if they were taking a test in school.

One part of the interview process was a completely random question. I would ask them a question to which there was no definitive answer, something un-Googleable, un-phone-a-friendable. For example, "How much gasoline is used in a day by American automobiles?" There is no single correct answer to these kinds of questions, simply because it's impossible to gather the data accurately. And to be honest, I had no interest in the correct answer anyway. What I was curious about was how my potential interns approached the problem. Did they turn to their computers and fire up a search engine? Did they sweat anxiously over their notebooks and calculators?

What I was *actually* looking for was the process by which they got to their answer. How many people in the United States? Average size of a family household? How many cars per house? Average time or distance for a commute? Average MPG for a car? I was usually amazed at how few students could do this, how few students know what questions to ask to get to the answer. Frankly, I would have loved for one of these best-of-the-best students to look me in the eye and ask, "Why do you want to know?"

WHY THIS MATTERS

What's the worst that can happen if you rely on old or obvious answers you know to be true? Consider the Deepwater Horizon explosion, a disaster that devastated both the environment and the people who rely on the clean waters and healthy bioflora for their living.

If you build thousands of floating oil platforms in the middle of a hurricane-prone body of water, it's possible that something could go wrong. So it would make sense to have a strategy in place to deal with these possibilities. However, BP seemed to operate under the common assumption that someone who has "the answer" is smarter than the one who asks questions. As a result, they already had their answers, both to the questions of *How do we prevent a catastrophic accident?* and *What do we do if one happens?* Yet their answers were based on what had worked in the past, both for BP and the oil industry. Something went wrong, and none of the answers worked.

BP is not alone, though. History is full of people who chose to assume that their plans would unfold smoothly and were shocked to find them derailed by an unexpected problem. Imagine if BP had asked itself, *What are the industry assumptions about safety and standards? What if they prove to no longer be true? I know that a blowout isn't possible on this rig, but what if one happened anyway? What would we do?* Imagine if BP had asked these questions and took an unpleasant answer—*A massive, devastating blowout is possible*—seriously. Would they have looked more seriously into innovative ways of containing oil? Would they have innovated better testing of the well design to prevent the blowout from even happening? It's impossible to know, because they believed that they'd never have to face those problems. If your company faces its challenges—whether those posed by customers or competitors—in the same way, you could find yourself in a similarly devastating stage of damage control.

HOW I'M GOING TO HELP YOU

In 2005, I became the vice president and chief technology officer for Hewlett-Packard's $40 billion (fiscal 2010) Personal Systems Group.[7] The role included being responsible for long-range strategic planning, research, and development for the company's PC product lines, including mobile devices, notebooks, desktops, and workstations. When I started in this role, I created and became the leader of the Innovation Program Office for HP.

The simplest truth is that I'm all about *ideas*. It's the job of the Innovation Program Office to make sure that the ideas HP needs to stay on top of its game keep on coming. In order to do so, the team must constantly generate great ideas, figure out which ones will work, and execute the best of them. *I love this*. I love seeing the look in someone's eyes when an idea comes together. It's a rush to see a technology that would have been considered science fiction five years ago rolled out to a worldwide audience.

HP—like all of Silicon Valley—is in a constant battle to stay on top. Yes, it has the biggest market share in the PC industry today, but who knows what could happen tomorrow.[8] All it takes is for a few missed opportunities by senior management, a badly thought-out product, and suddenly you're the next Silicon Graphics—a once-brilliant company that has made the fatal mistake of assuming what was true yesterday will stay true tomorrow. Or you're Friendster, a company that could have been a contender but completely misunderstood what its users wanted from it and withered away to make room for the company that *did* get it: Facebook.

One of my favorite activities is to get out there and engage with our customers. In this capacity, and also in my own personal life, I meet businesspeople from a wide range of industries—and at all levels of seniority—on a daily basis. As we talk I hear their concerns about the future of their organizations and their own careers.

Over the last decade, the concept of the "creative economy" has overtaken the older paradigm of the information-based economy. The basic idea behind the creative economy is simple: The most important skill is now no longer simply having knowledge, but demonstrating the ability to use that knowledge to come up with new and great ideas. The booming creative economy is starving for people with the energy, confidence, and ability to innovate. *Knowing the old answers* no longer impresses; having the ability to come up with the new answers does.

If you aren't already moving confidently in the creative economy, you need to learn how to do so. I understand that this might not be easy. Perhaps you have the secret fear that you will get derailed in your pursuit of a great innovation, maybe betting on the wrong idea, or saying no to an opportunity that ends up being a smash. Perhaps you worry that you'll never generate the momentum to achieve meaningful success in your professional life. Or worse, that you'll have great ideas that you can never quite get out of the starting gate and turn into something real.

Perhaps what keeps you up at night is the thought that you have a competitor who is one step closer than you are to getting their version of your make-or-break idea out in the marketplace. You know that you need to move fast before they do, but you have doubts that are paralyzing you. The days are ticking by, yet you can't pull the trigger because you're simply not sure what the right move is. One day you'll wake up to news that they've launched; your brilliant innovation is now perceived as the first imitator of *their* brilliant innovation. Even if you catch up or outperform them, you'll always know you could have been first. Regardless of your specific fear, my goal in this book is to arm you with the same sort of tools that I use to help my team, as well as my clients, to create the solutions they need for success—and to enjoy the thrill of innovation.

THE KILLER QUESTIONS SYSTEM

Throughout the course of my career, I've developed a personal approach that has allowed me to find innovative ideas in areas where my competitors never thought to look and come up with products that my customers never knew they wanted. Perhaps more important, it's given me freedom. By using this technique I've not only been able to generate a continuous flow of ideas for the companies I've worked for, but more important, I've had confidence that these ideas are good.

Learning the skills I'll teach in this book is crucial; individuals who know how to phrase and ask the right questions can reveal things that others have missed. They can shift the day-to-day realities of how an organization perceives itself, the services or products it offers, and the people it hopes to sell them to. These shifts in belief and assumption are critical if you want to get—and stay—ahead. Yet there is no cultural tradition for learning how to overcome a reliance on your past experiences—those "obvious" ideas that relate more to the past than the future.

I've spent the past ten years writing and developing a system of generating new ideas that lead to radical innovations, and this system uses what I call the "Killer Questions." In the coming chapters, I'll guide you through the process of asking the Killer Questions about your business, focusing on your customers, your services or products, and how you conduct your business. I'll also talk about one of my core beliefs—that innovation without execution is a hobby. Part of being an innovator is having the ability to get your ideas out of your head or your notebook and into the prototype, testing, and eventually the marketplace phases. This process will show you a proven way to plan and execute your best ideas.

||||||||||||||

You may not think of yourself as an innovator, but you have just as much potential as the person who has the title of "the creative." You simply haven't had access to a system that will guide you through the process of generating and executing great ideas.

We don't know how our world is going to change, and we don't know how our industry is going to evolve. But as long as you continue to ask good questions and get beyond the obvious answers, you keep the momentum of discovery and innovation going—and you open yourself up to continual discovery. It's my goal to give you the techniques to generate truly great, innovative ideas and the confidence to know you've picked the strongest of these ideas to bet on.

So be fearless and believe that you can come up with the types of ideas that will propel you to the next level of your career. And as you progress toward great ideas and innovations, I want you to stay in touch.

I currently use my podcasts at philmckinney.com, and Twitter handle @philmckinney to communicate with other innovators, and I also have an e-mail address, feedback@philmckinney.com, where you can reach out to me with ideas and stories about your experience with my method. The podcasts and Killer Questions themselves are licensed under Creative Commons, which allows for nonderivative, noncommercial use with attribution source, so please feel free to share them with your coworkers, friends, and family (just be sure to mention where you found them!). I hope that my various platforms will become a way for you to communicate directly with other innovators as well.

PART I

PREPARING FOR INNOVATION

CHAPTER 1

Why Questions Matter

Judge a man by his questions, rather than by his answers.[1]
—Voltaire

O ne day when my kids were still little, I was sitting in the car with my daughter Tara. She was about four years old at the time, and as we drove down the street she noticed the curb along the side of the road and got curious about it. Suddenly I was fielding question after question about curbs. Why did we need them? What would happen if there weren't a curb? What were they made of? What's so good about concrete? What's concrete made of? Every parent has had a similar experience, but that afternoon sticks in my mind because it was one of the first times I turned to one of my kids and said, "You know what, I don't know the answer to that. Why don't you find out for both of us?"

When we got home, Tara ran to her room and started to try to figure out the answers to the questions. She was excited to find the answers *because* I hadn't known them, and I'd passed on the responsibility of figuring them out to her. What I realized at that moment was that the natural curiosity of kids gets lost over time. As adults, we use our education and past experiences to solve the problems we face rather than relying on questions. It's these historical assumptions of what works that prevents organizations from generating new ideas. After all, you can't change your core beliefs about your organization or industry unless you change something in your perspective about your business, your industry, your customers, or yourself. Think of it this way: If you want to start generating new output, you first need new input. And the only way to get new input is to either find new sources of information and inspiration *or* find new ways of looking at the same existing information you've been looking at for years.

There are many ways to generate new input, but the most effective is to learn to ask the kinds of questions that can lead you to a real discovery. This is true both of the kinds of questions you ask other people, and the ones you pose to yourself. It's also true both in the straightforward semantic sense (*you need to be able to use words in order to phrase an effective question*) and in the larger philosophical sense (*you need to know how, why, and when to ask the right kinds of questions*).

In that moment with Tara, I realized there was a difference that questions can make in the discovery process. Learning how to effectively phrase, ask, and use questions became one of the pillars of my innovation philosophy.

THE POWER OF QUESTIONS

I've been fascinated by the power of questions, either good or bad, for my entire professional life. The more I thought about them, the more I began to notice how people used them. I started to see how some people had the innate ability to formulate and pose questions that propelled others to make investigations and discoveries of their own, and some people had the less-desirable ability to shut their listeners down with bad questions, poorly asked. I believe that a good question is one that causes people to really think before they answer it, and one that reveals answers that had previously eluded them. I began to think more about how an individual could learn to ask good questions and avoid the pitfalls of asking bad questions. I also wondered whether a poor questioning technique could become a crutch, something that allows you to believe you are accomplishing something positive, when in fact you are doing the opposite.

As I listened to my children ask challenging questions of each other, I realized I had taught them a profound skill. By passing on a love of questions, I'd shared my belief in the importance of getting out there and proactively making our own discoveries about the world. My children weren't afraid or ashamed of not knowing an answer; instead they were invigorated by the process of finding it. I compared this attitude to the converse one that I'd seen throughout my career, namely employees who felt compelled to agree with their superiors or believed that saying "I don't know" would adversely affect their career. These men and women would have benefitted greatly from simply being empowered to admit that they didn't know how to ask good questions, and to seek out the relevant answers.

HOW QUESTIONS WORK

If you are going to start thinking about questions, it is helpful to understand what a fundamental shift it was for humans to learn how to ask them. According to primatologists, the great apes can understand and answer simple questions.[2] However, unlike humans, a great ape has never proven that it can *ask* questions. Nor has any other creature, at least in any way that's recognizable to us. Your dog can make his desires known to you, but he can't actually ask you to take him for a walk. All he can do is wag his tail and hope you figure out for yourself what he needs and wants. As a result, the ability to form a question might be the key cognitive transition that separates apes, and all other beings, from mankind. The desire to ask a question shows a higher level of thought, one that accepts that your own knowledge of a situation isn't complete or perfect.

The natural world has some great examples of why this ability to think inquisitively is a critical survival skill. Have you ever seen an army ant mill? Army ants are an aggressive and nomadic variety of ant that moves constantly, unlike the ants that your kids display between glass at a science fair.[3] Army ants have the innate drive to follow the ant in front of them, which makes sense if you are a member of a colony on the move. This instinct allows them to move cohesively and maintain their colony, but it is also their greatest flaw. Every so often the head of an army-ant column runs into its tail. The ant who was leading the way sees an ant in front of it and the genetic programming kicks in; he goes from leader to follower, and the column of ants turns into a circle, or mill. The ants have no ability to break free from the circle, and they keep walking until they die.[4] The only thing that can save them is if there is a "broken" ant in the mill, one whose programming to "follow the ant in front" is missing or flawed in some way. This ant will step out of formation, the ant behind him follows, the mill is broken, and the colony saved.

Recent research validates this idea that "brokenness" is a key element to a questioning and creative spirit. Scientists have started to prove what most people in the tech or other creative spheres already know: If you want to be innovative, it helps to be a little bit "different." True genius seems to come when extremely intelligent people have high levels of cognitive disinhibition. In other words, they are naturally smart people who don't filter the information they absorb and have the mental agility to process and use this information in an organized way.[5]

Now, I want to be clear that I am using terms like "brokenness" or "different" in the most positive way; after all, the core of this book is learning how to use questions to think differently—to cause your own version of cognitive disinhibition—even if it's not your automatic instinct. I believe that anyone can develop and harness this power through the use of provocative questioning and discovery.

BAD QUESTIONS, GOOD QUESTIONS

The more I started to look at questions and how essential they are to fostering creativity and innovation, the more I realized that there are *bad* questions and there are *good* questions. And within those good questions, some just aren't relevant to the process of ideation. The key to using this book is to develop the ability to separate the good, useful questions from the bad ones. Here's a quick guide:

Tag Questions

During my search, I realized that some of the most important questions to avoid are ones that don't really ask for a response at all. For example, tag questions. Tag questions are statements that appear to be questions, but don't allow for any kind of answer except agreement. A tag question is really a declarative statement turned into a question, and used to get validation for the speaker's "answer." Family members, authority figures, or executives who want to appear to care about the opinion of another person, but really want their instructions carried out without discussion, often favor tag questions. A tag question can show that the speaker is either overly confident of his or her beliefs, or so insecure that he has to bully others into agreeing with him. Either way, his phrasing of the question shows that he is not willing to consider an alternative point of view. You're not actually being asked for an opinion, simply for a confirmation that you agree with them. When lawyers use tag questions in a legal setting, they are sometimes referred to as leading the witness, the questions being posed in such a way as to guide the person in a desired direction; that is how you should think of a tag question as well.[6]

That presentation was fantastic, wasn't it?
The new brochure will be based on the last version, won't it?

Tag questions can be incredibly damaging both to an individual and to an organization because they shut down the creative process. Say you've been tasked to come up with a new product but your boss asks you to verify that "the new concepts that you are coming up with aren't going to be *too* different from the old ones, right?" By asking this question, she has taken away any power from your team to go out and do something really new. The fundamental point of asking a question is to get information, input, or ideas. Any question that restricts people from feeling free to honestly answer it is offensive; it reduces the quality of information you're going to get and makes the person being questioned feel that they are being dismissed.

Typically, a person who uses tag questions is a manager who believes that his role is to be directive. However, by doing so he misses out on the potential power of a team. Look at the way you communicate with your coworkers; if you find yourself asking tag questions, ask yourself why. Do you doubt their ability to come up with their own answers, or do you already have an answer in mind that you would like them to validate? If you are simply looking to get validation for what you already want or believe, this runs counter to every philosophy about generating new and innovative ideas. When I'm working with a team, I'll always use a series of questions to see what they come up with, even when I already have an idea in my mind of what the answer may be. Even if I give them that answer, it's always presented as a challenge for them to come up with something better.

Factual vs. Investigative

After more searching and studying, I came up with two basic categories of good questions: factual and investigative. So, what are the differences between them? The objective of a factual question is to get information: "Do you want coffee or tea?" "How many units did we sell last week?" "Is there gas in the car?" You may not know the immediate answer to a factual question, but you know how to find it. There is no real discovery required beyond expressing your opinion, making a call, or looking at the gas gauge. Factual questions serve an important purpose in allowing us to communicate with one another and exchange information. They are limited in their ability to do anything more nuanced than gather information.

An investigative question, on the other hand, cannot be answered with a yes or a no and is much more useful for our purposes. By definition, it is a divergent question, meaning that there is more than one correct answer (unlike factual questions). It cannot be answered with one phone call or a quick check at some stats or figures, and it forces us to investigate all of the possibilities.

The Socratic Method

So how do you generate some good investigative questions? One of my starting points is the Socratic Method. Socratic questions are, in their simplest definition, questions that challenge you to justify your beliefs about a subject, often over a series of questions, rather than responding with an answer that you've been taught is "correct." A well-phrased series of Socratic questions challenges you to think about why you believe your "answer" to be correct, and to supply some sort of evidence to back up your beliefs. At the same time, a Socratic set of questions doesn't assume you are right or wrong.

When using this method, Socrates would lead his listener to a deeper understanding of his own beliefs and how and why he justified them. When a student attempted to fall back on a belief prefaced by "I've heard it said that such and such is true," Socrates would gently push further, asking the student what he himself actually thought, until the student finally got to the heart of what he thought and believed. Socrates would also find contradictions in a student's expressed belief, and ask him questions that forced him to consider these contradictions. Ultimately, Socrates's goal was to help the student unveil his own thoughts and his own beliefs, and see them clearly for the first time. It was only by finally articulating one's own thoughts and bringing them into "open air," he felt, that the student could fully understand the depths of his own knowledge.[7]

Socrates believed that knowledge was possible, but believed that the first step toward knowledge was a recognition of one's ignorance. It's the same in the idea-generation process; the first step to freeing yourself to find innovations is to recognize that the knowledge you currently have is insufficient, and that you need to go out and discover new information that will lead to new products or concepts.

My interest in the Socratic Method, and the glaring gap I found between Socrates's method of teaching with questions and the way innovation and ideation is "taught" today, started me down the path of searching for specific questions that would challenge others to find opportunities for new ideas—questions I now call Killer Questions. It took me a while to determine them, but in the end I hit upon the old engineering standby: Find something that works, and figure out why.

THE KILLER QUESTIONS

I started writing the Killer Questions when I was in my short-lived "retirement" early in 2001. As I relaxed in the Virginia countryside, my mind started to flash back to various experiences I'd had during my working life. Over the course of the preceding twenty years, I'd seen dozens of highly innovative products and ideas come to market. I started to ask myself a broad range of investigative questions about how and why successful products work. The most important issue seemed to be that of understanding the thought process that led to these discoveries.

One memory from my old career jumped into my head. In late 1994, I was sitting in a limo in a traffic jam in Bangkok. We'd been in traffic for half an hour, and I had only twenty-eight minutes until a critical meeting started. The limo was cooled to American standards, and the German steel and glass kept the chaotic noise and rush of people outside the doors. At twenty-three minutes, I started to feel a little anxious; the car wasn't moving, but the clock was. I tapped the driver on the shoulder and tried to communicate my sense of urgency, but he wasn't interested. He knew we weren't going anywhere soon, and I wasn't doing myself any favors by worrying about it. At eighteen minutes to go, I jumped out of the car and hailed a motorcycle taxi.

Thai motorbike taxis are 125ccs of terror. I've ridden motorcycles before, but I can honestly say I've never felt as close to disaster as I did then, riding pillion on a tiny Honda motorcycle, going flat-out through the sweltering heat with my briefcase clutched to my chest. As we swerved through the tuk-tuks, pedestrians, and stalled cars, I found myself thinking about the difference between the super-cheap motorcycles that swamp the streets of Southeast Asia and the ultraluxe bikes manufactured by companies like Harley-Davidson. How had something that started as cheap and efficient transportation for the American working man evolved into a big-ticket luxury item? Who was the first person who thought, *Can we take our mass-produced product and customize it? What if we stop trying to make our product cheaper, and go the other way? What happens if we double, maybe triple, the price and make this a luxury item instead?*

I thought about the contrast between a very mainstream product (the inexpensive motorcycle) and the one that had breakout success (Harley-Davidson). Could I reverse-engineer this evolution of a product, and figure out the question that could lead someone to come up with that idea? And if I could reverse the thought process that led to innovative products and find the questions that might have generated these ideas, would those same questions lead to new discoveries and new products in the future? With these questions in mind, I wrote down this first question—*Who is passionate about your product or something it relates to? Why or why not?*—on a blank white index card and resolved to keep doing so each time I came across other questions that seemed to spark especially good ideas.

||||||||||||||

As the months passed, these cards started to multiply, so I decided to put together a card deck that I kept in a big binder clip. Before each innovation workshop I'd flip quickly through the set and pull out a few questions to ask the participants. I constantly tested the questions in workshops to see which questions would generate the best ideas. I kept the ones that worked and tossed the ones that didn't. Sometimes

I realized that a question had the potential to spark a good idea, but I had worded it poorly, so I experimented with the question by adjusting the language.

After a year or so, the walls in my home office were filled with Killer Questions. They were scrawled on index cards and stuffed in shoeboxes or pinned up on the wall. The sheer volume was driving my wife crazy. That's when I realized I needed to formalize the system, strip it down to the most effective questions, and develop a way to organize and use them. You'll learn more as we go through the book, but for now know that the Questions are divided into three categories: (1) *Who your customer is*, (2) *What you sell them*, and (3) *How your organization operates*. Each category has roughly twenty questions to date, and more are constantly being tested and added to the card deck.

So, is the list static? No. The key to the value of the Killer Questions is that new ones are continuously being discovered. Sometimes I get questions sent to me by the listeners to my podcast. Other times, I come up with new ones in support of an upcoming workshop, or they come to me when I'm reading a story in the Sunday paper.

The questions that I keep are ones that trigger something for someone. Did a new question cause a listener or reader to see something differently about their product, customer, or organization? Did it spark a broader examination of how they were doing something, and why?

One of my favorite killer questions is one of the simplest: "What do my potential customers not like about the buying experience?" This is a classic Killer Question; on first glance, it seems obvious, but once people start to think about it, they realize they've never actually asked that of themselves or their business. In fact, the overwhelming majority of organizations do not measure or track what their potential customers *dislike* about their buying experience, instead choosing to focus on issues with the product or support. In reality, this question is almost impossible to measure. Think about it. How would you find a potential customer who had such a bad buying experience that they didn't buy your product? Digging into what the potential customer actively dislikes about buying a product can be a gold mine, especially when your competitors aren't making that investigation.

The only way to capture this information is to be right there, observing your customers in action as they select or reject your product. You can't e-mail or follow up with them because you don't know who they are; they didn't buy your product. You have to catch them in the moment and ask them right then and there. The question gives you a broad area to look at: It could be a brand, sales, marketing, or merchandising issue. The point of a Killer Question is to challenge you to look at things in a new and different way. A really good Killer Question will leave you surprised by the answer.

Do I Really Need Killer Questions?

You may be wondering if you really need to change the way you think about questions. What's wrong with staying on the current course and speed within your organization? Well, for one thing, the world is changing around you. Without a change in the way you see your customers, product, and organization, you will fall into the assumptions and rules that define your industry. Think of the ants, endlessly walking in a circle. They are doing what they are supposed to do, and are in perfect agreement about the correctness of doing it. However, their uniformity will destroy them, unless that different ant comes along to break the rules.

The Killer Questions I'll share later in the book will help you become the "broken ant" your organization needs you to be. However, before we get to them, we need to take a look at the forces within organizations that can either snuff out or kindle the innovative spark they're intended to create. First, we'll look at how existing assumptions about your organization and industry can get in the way of great idea generation and new products or concepts, as well as the jolts that can either disrupt or encourage innovation, depending on how and why they happen. Then we'll look at the people—I call them the corporate antibodies—who impulsively attack and destroy the new ideas your company so desperately needs. If you can get past the assumptions, manage the jolts, and neutralize the corporate antibodies, your company will be ready to use the Killer Questions to their maximum effect.

Now's the time to grab a notebook and pen and start to jot down anything you notice that causes you to think differently. Read along, but remember this is a two-way street; it's crucial that you jot down anything that strikes a chord, or simply flashes quickly across your mind. Keep in mind that the questions in this book use the word "product," but the questions can also be used for "services," or "solutions," as well. I use "product" to mean anything that your company generates for the purpose of selling to or servicing the needs of a customer.

CHAPTER 2

Questioning Your Assumptions, Managing Your Jolts

U nderstanding how questions work is one thing, but understanding why you need to ask them is another. This chapter is, first, about looking at the core beliefs, your assumptions, and asking, "Why do I believe this, and is it still true today?" Second, it is about preparing for the challenges that these assumptions inevitably face from external forces I call "jolts."

I'll get into more detail about jolts a bit later in the chapter, but for now it's enough to know that a jolt is an unexpected event that comes along and rattles everything you know to be true about your business. It is usually a sudden and radical changing of the rules and can come from many sources, including competitors, government regulators, or sudden and unanticipated disasters. The best way to avoid these jolts is to actively use questions to drive innovation, rather than waiting to come up with a good idea when things have gotten out of your control. If you constantly challenge your assumptions, you'll be more likely to prevent some jolts and to effectively handle the ones you can't avoid.

ASSUMPTION BUSTING

Every year, I travel around the world giving workshops and motivational talks on innovation. I enjoy doing this; I'm a naturally curious person, and there's always something interesting to observe and learn from these speaking dates. Often, I'll walk into an auditorium full of people wondering if they will learn anything new that they can apply to their job. Sometimes the audience is comfortable and complacent. They feel they have it all figured out. Of course, when a company is full of people who "know best," that's when I can really get in there and kick-start a big change in a short period of time. Why? Because these people feel safe both within their organization and within their overall industry. This sense of safety can feel pleasant and positive. The problem is that this feeling is a by-product of certainty, and certainty can lead to dangerous assumptions. These assumptions can be fallacies about who you are, what you do, and how you do it. They can become barriers that prevent people from asking the kinds of questions that challenge the obvious, and are necessary to continue to move your organization and your own career forward.

So, when I'm up there on a podium, in front of hundreds and sometimes thousands of employees, the first thing I do is challenge them to *see* their assumptions. To really get a grasp on those old, obvious answers that their business has clung to for years. It's only when you can see those assumptions that you can let go of them and move forward on the path toward new ideas and breakthrough innovations.

Occasionally, the employees who attend these kinds of workshops have already seen the change that needs to happen in their company. However, when they've tried to address it with management, they aren't taken seriously. In some cases, senior management needs to hear these ideas from an outside expert in order to accept that the concerns are valid. Now, this can be very flawed logic; after all, who knows the strengths and failings of an organization better than the people who work with (or around) them every day? The reality is that we all seek external validation for our actions, and in these situations I'm brought in as an outsider precisely because I can validate what employees within the organization already believe. I can be blunt; what are they going to do, fire me? Other times, the role of an outsider is to discover problems that people are too busy working to think about.

I use this platform as the outsider to help companies move past the "business as usual" mentality that handcuffs them to what has worked for them in the past. The first step is to help them determine what their assumptions are—and teach them how to challenge the ones that hold them back.

Be Your Own Outsider

Of course, the problem with trying to be the "outsider" is that most of us aren't outsiders. We are inside—inside our company, our industry, or our organization. There's a delicate balancing act between being the person who can speak the confrontational, difficult truths, and the person who can speak these same truths in a way that doesn't risk their career or job.

The funny thing is that HP brought in outsiders to talk about innovation, even though I was regularly giving innovation workshops at American Express, Roche, Kroger, Televisa, and many other companies. Even my own company needed to hear the innovation message from an outside voice. It is important to understand that companies, and the people who run them, suffer from fear and uncertainty about change. They need a level of confidence that there is an approach that can work and that the risk of change isn't as big as they think it is. A company will bring me in because they want to hear how it's done at other organizations, and once they've heard how others have discovered and executed breakthrough innovations, some of the fear goes away. It is replaced by a sense of "If they can do it, so can we"—in other words, confidence. Don't take it as a negative if your company brings an outsider in; they are simply looking for validation that the risk of failure isn't as bad as they think it is.

No matter what your situation, whether you are an insider or an outsider, you need to become the voice that challenges yesterday's answers. Think about the characteristics that make outsiders valuable to an organization. They are the people who have the perspective to see problems that the insiders are too close to really notice. They are the ones who have the freedom to point out these problems and critique them without risking their job or their career. Part of adopting an outsider mentality is forcing yourself to look around your organization with this disassociated, less emotional perspective. If you didn't know your coworkers and feel bonded to them by your shared experiences, what would you think of them? If you hadn't invested years of your life on a project, how would you assess its potential and future viability? You may not have the job security or confidence to speak your mind to management, but you can make these "outsider" assessments of your organization on your own and use what you determine to advance your career. You don't have to go out with an ax and chop down the "golden assumptions"—those core rules that drive your organization— right away. You can start smaller and take aim at less-central tenets of your business. Once you have a sense of how your ideas are being received, you can move on to the bigger, "obvious" assumptions.

Getting Past the Obvious First Answer

In many cases the comfortable people in my workshops are really "fake-comfortable." They've been successful in the past, and they use these successes as a guide for how to move forward in the present and future. They are understandably reluctant to let go of that buoy and try to swim to another; who knows what's waiting out there to bite them? My role in this situation is to show them that they can't do things the same way forever, and that there is a process to get them past the sharks to the other ideas floating out on the waves.

Individuals who feel comfortable need to be shaken out of their complacency to realize how narrow their vision is. The people who are uncertain about how to meet the changing realities of their business need to feel confident in their ability to do so, and to be reminded that they have the courage to try. But this requires an ability to step out of our own biases and to identify the "safe" assumptions and rules our industry operates under. In order to identify these safe assumptions, I run a series of warm-up exercises in my workshops. In the same way that a runner warms up and stretches before a race, these exercises help wake you up, stretch your brain, and recognize that you might have biases in place.

EXERCISE 1: A DIVISION PROBLEM

What is half of thirteen?
Write down your answer.

Did you write down 6.5? Great, there's no denying that is a correct answer to the question. Now, did you stop there? If you did, you are in the majority. In this exercise, there is an assumption of what is meant by the word "half." The point is to ignore that "taught" answer—to ignore the assumptions—and to look beyond the obvious. If you kept going, perhaps you wrote down Thir/teen. Or maybe you thought about how thirteen is written in Roman numerals—XIII. If you divided that in half visually it would be XI/II, or 11/2. Did you round up your answer and write 6/7? Thirteen is also a Fibonacci number, and 2.2 is in the middle of the sequence of numbers between zero and thirteen. There are thirteen cards in a suit, and dividing the numbered cards would give you 5.5. Once you start looking for alternative answers, there are tons of ways to respond to this question. Some solutions are more logical than others, and some are purely whimsical. But the point of this exercise is to learn to look beyond the obvious—and to see that there are answers that are beyond the obvious. We're not looking for logical and sensible answers. Instead, what we're doing is learning different ways to look at the question. Come up with a list of your own answers. Have fun, and don't worry too much if your responses feel like a bit of a stretch.

This exercise is about realizing you have a language bias; you know what words mean, how they should be used, and how to respond to them. But the reality is that many words can be subjective in either meaning or interpretation. Do you ever make similar assumptions about how to use words when you are communicating with your coworkers, customers, friends, and family? Do they do it? How might this assumption get in the way of effective discovery and idea generation?

EXERCISE 2: WHY ARE MANHOLE COVERS ROUND?

Why are most manhole covers round? I'm guessing that you've seen many manhole covers, perhaps noticed their surprisingly intricate and sometimes quite beautiful designs, but not given them much thought beyond that cursory glance. The basic principle of a manhole cover is the result of some simple but inspired design. A manhole cover works best if it is round. Why? What is it about the manhole cover's physical appearance that is critical to its functionality? The answer is simple and based on geometry: There is only one shape that prevents a manhole cover from falling through a manhole—a circle.

The manhole cover question is about realizing that you have a visual bias. It's easy to look at a familiar object like this and impose your own sense of order on it, depending on your particular interests or ways of processing information.

EXERCISE 3: WHAT'S IN A BIC?

For the final exercise, I pull an empty Bic ballpoint pen barrel out of my briefcase and hold it up in front of the group. I give them a minute to write down ten possible uses for the pen. I've gotten responses that range from a tracheotomy tube to a small-bore blow dart.

This exercise shows the natural evolution of taking an everyday object you never really think about and building upon it to create a whole new product. Building upon an existing idea doesn't minimize the importance or relevance of that original idea; it's simply part of the natural flow of innovation. Part of the pen exercise is helping people understand that nothing is ever really "new," and that you shouldn't discount an idea because it's not 100 percent original.

The Bic pen test is also about historical bias. Once something has been assigned a certain property or function, or been identified as "doing X," you assume that's what it does; a pen is a pen is a pen. But the potential uses for products evolve over time, and you don't want to miss a new application, either for a product or the separate elements that go into a product.

|||||||||||||||||

The point of all these exercises is that you don't want to stop at the first obvious answer or get hung up on an assumption about what constitutes a "correct" response. The half-of-thirteen question asks you to think of assumptions you may be making about what a word or phrase means. How is this assumption affecting how you think about the problem or opportunity in front of you?

The manhole cover question is designed to make you think about form and function and how you might be neglecting, overlooking, or misunderstanding it in your own design process or overall product function. When I bring this question up in a workshop, I want people to look beyond the obvious (design) to the less obvious (function). Are there other simple visual lessons out there that you should be learning from?

The Bic pen reminds you to look at whether you've made needlessly limiting assumptions about what a component or element of a product might be used for. Are you actively looking for other ways to use your existing products and offer them to new consumer groups or to your existing customers in a new way?

WHAT ARE YOUR ASSUMPTIONS?

The following questions are designed to help you discover the rules and assumptions under which your organization and industry operates. I want you to use them to start unraveling the assumptions you have about your business, your industry, and your own role in the marketplace.

The key here is to be able to get the assumptions that run around in everyone's head out on paper. Only then can you shed the old constraints that held you back and look at new opportunities. By getting these assumptions out in the open, you have permission to challenge them in the context of new ideas.

What are the assumptions under which my industry operates?

In order to move beyond your assumptions about your industry, you need to first be able to identify them. This is harder than it seems; our assumptions are so ingrained in us that they appear less a personal belief and more a universal truth. So, what are yours? What are the "rules" about how your industry is structured? How often do you reconsider what the rules are about what your customers like or don't like, or what the rules are about how you operate?

Since deciding to write a book, I've started to think a lot about the assumptions that the publishing industry operates under. As I work on *Beyond the Obvious* in early 2011, I'm already thinking about all the possible ways we can make the book a unique experience for the reader. I hope that, in the near future, books can begin to transform into a multidimensional experience. Perhaps publishers will be able to find new ways to publish books that will literally bring books like *Beyond the Obvious* to life and allow readers to communicate with authors, and one another, in a real-time way.

When I did my rounds of meetings with all the potential editors and publishers, I was asked again and again, "*What are the killer questions we should be asking ourselves? How do we change our industry in the face of new media?*" My reply was to ask the same basic questions I discussed with my publishing team for *Beyond the Obvious*. What is a book? What does the book of tomorrow look like? How are we going to deliver these books to our readers? How are we going to apply the lessons learned from the changes in the music industry?

The point is that publishers are experimenting with ways they can reshape what a book is, and how they sell it to readers. People clearly still want books, but they don't want to buy them and read them in the same ways they used to. Simply transferring content over to e-books won't satisfy readers for long.

I'm very curious to see how the fundamental manner in which a reader *experiences* and *uses* a book will change over the next few years. I also wonder whether books will continue to be sold as fixed, final texts. Think about it: With the exception of textbooks or reference books (or minor tweaks in subsequent editions of other types of books), we assume that books *will stay the same* once they are published. Yet this doesn't reflect the way people consume and interact with information now. How will publishers evolve *how* they sell—beyond just saying "let's go digital"—and create an evolving experience for the reader? Who says a book needs to remain fixed and static? Maybe the books of the future should be fluid and ever-evolving? If an author can revise his e-book after the publication date, why shouldn't he?

It's an interesting thought. I'm an innovation guy, yet here I am, working in a medium that is more than two thousand years old. I'd love it if *Beyond the Obvious* could become a focal point around which innovators, kids, businesspeople, hobbyists, students, and educators could debate, swap ideas, and spur one another on to be more creative and dig deeper. Perhaps one day readers will actually contribute to the book, enhancing its quality and adding to its value over the years. We'll see.

FURTHER QUESTIONS

Why is your industry structured the way it is?

What are the rules for how your industry interacts with customers, manufacturers, distributors, retailers, etc.?

What would be the effect on your business if these assumptions changed? Which of these assumptions could you change that would radically alter your position in the industry?

What are the assumptions under which my company operates?

My dad worked his entire adult life at a company called Cincinnati
Milacron. The company was founded in 1889 and started off as a little
shop that made machine tools.[1] Eventually, they became the world's
largest manufacturer of machine tools.

In the 1970s, the Japanese came in and began to build machines
that looked almost identical to the machines that Milacron was famous for. The Japanese were gaining a reputation for duplicating
what existing US businesses were doing, but offering a significantly
cheaper version of their products.[2] Now, this would be an alarming situation for any business, but the Mil's management had confidence in the quality of their products. It had taken them a hundred
years to refine and perfect what they built, and they were renowned
for the features and functions of their machines. They felt certain
that their new rivals would never be able to catch up and replicate
their full feature set. And they were correct on that score; the Japanese versions of Milacron's products never had the same capabilities. What the Mil failed to account for was something that the
Japanese understood: their customers' priorities had changed. The
Mil thought their trump card was their quality workmanship and
rich feature set. They believed that if customers had to pay a premium
for the features, they would. They didn't see that their customers
were feeling pressed by cheap imports and the changing realities of
the economy. Price was beginning to win in the battle between cost
and features.

Fast-forward from 1970 to 1998. Cincinnati Milacron lost so
much market share in the machine tool business that they sold off the
machine tool division.[3]

So what went wrong? Cincinnati Milacron was a market leader.
However, their sense of history and pride in their work and reputation
worked against them. Their leadership assumed that they understood
the rules of their industry and how a successful company operated.
They knew who their customers were and what they wanted, and they

weren't going to waste time wondering if the Japanese had sensed a change in the marketplace that they themselves were ignoring. This certainty blinded them to the reality that their industry was indeed changing; their customers were feeling the pinch of cheap foreign-made products that needed lower-cost machines and couldn't afford Milacron's price premium.

FURTHER QUESTIONS

Why is your organization organized the way it is?

What are the rules your organization operates under?

Is the organization operating the same today as it did in the past?

What are the assumptions about your customers, products, and how you operate?

THE JOLTS

If assumptions keep you safe, comfortable, and stagnant, then jolts are their counterpart. Jolts are the earthquakes and the tsunamis, metaphorical and occasionally literal, that you either don't or can't see coming. Jolts can be terrifying; one day you wake up and a fundamental assumption about how you do business has crumbled away. Its absence can leave a hole in your understanding about what you do and how you do it. However, learning how to navigate the jolts is a key element in the innovation process. Look at it this way: A big jolt will put a hole into how you do things, but also in how your competitors do things. If you already have the "jolts happen" mind-set in place, you can leapfrog over your competitors who may be in numb denial about the unexpected shift. This is an opportunity for you, and you need to recognize it and act fast.

So, a key part of using the Killer Questions is to challenge your organization to prepare for unpredictable events that can seriously affect your business. It is also about opening your eyes to ways in which you can do something so unexpected, so jolting, that it throws off your competition, thereby giving you a competitive advantage.

There are two kinds of jolts that can affect you. The first is the unexpected jolt, and the second is the competitive jolt. Notice I said "affect," not "damage" or "harm." Jolts can be devastating if you are unprepared to deal with them, and the nature of a jolt means that you won't see it coming. But a meaningful jolt can open up major opportunities if you have the fast reflexes and confidence to respond to them in a proactive way.

What are the unexpected jolts that could transform your business?

What's the worst-case scenario for you or your company? What situation is so dire that you *know* it will never happen? Something so unrealistic that it seems pointless to prepare for it? Consider Johnson & Johnson's situation in 1982, when seven people in the Chicago area, three from the same family, died after taking Tylenol capsules that had been tampered with by an unknown saboteur. Though an arrest was never made, a suspect was identified, and it seems likely the poisonings were part of a poorly conceived extortion attempt against Johnson & Johnson. More than 31 million bottles of product had to be recalled, and at one point police officers were driving through residential streets in Chicago using bullhorns to instruct people to throw away their Tylenol.

Johnson & Johnson, like all drug companies at the time, did not protect their product from saboteurs *because no one had ever tried to compromise their product before*. The packaging could be opened and resealed, the capsules could be easily pulled apart, tampered with, and reassembled. The Tylenol murders could have destroyed J & J, but they didn't. Why? Because Johnson & Johnson made bold moves and disregarded *how things had been done in the past*. In the space of a few months, Johnson & Johnson had a new imperative: We must protect our products and our customers from tampering. They ordered a $100 million recall and designed antitampering packaging that has since set the standard for the industry. They also realized they needed to phase out the easily compromised capsules in favor of caplets, though it took another scare in 1986 to pull the last capsules off the shelves.[4] Even so, for a company as large as J & J, this was swift action. So, what would be your Tylenol scare?

How can I create a jolt that will give me a competitive advantage?

Yahoo! is a good example of a company that was blindsided by a competitor making a quantum leap in improving their core product. In the late '90s, Yahoo! thought they had "search" in the bag. They developed a search feature where websites were rated by people who individually curated and ranked pages. Sure, it was laborious, but it allowed for accurate search results. Yahoo! never seemed to put serious thought into what would happen if a rival came up with a much better search engine. We know what happened next. A couple of guys from Stanford came up with the idea of automated page-ranking rather than human organization, and Google was born.[5]

That's a big shift. Yahoo! was essentially offering a very modern service (an Internet search engine) that was curated in a very traditional way (by humans). Google came along and said, "There is a better way to do this." They devised a system where the popularity of a page, and the number of links or views it garnered, decided what level of influence it had, and where it fell in a search listing.

Yahoo! was prepared for a competitor who could improve on their product, but they assumed they'd be dealing with an improvement of 5 or 10 percent. They were completely unprepared for a total change in how search results were gathered. Google then went on to develop an entirely new business model in terms of selling advertising, and the rest is history. Bear in mind that in 1999, Google was in negotiations to sell itself to Excite for less than a million dollars.[6] Things change fast, and knowing how to anticipate and (in some cases) create jolts can help you stay on top of unexpected changes. This question is about thinking about "what happens if our fundamental business changes, either for better or for worse?"

Take a few minutes and think about your personal history, and the history of your organization and industry. Have you ever experienced a jolt in either a negative or positive way? It's critical to understand that your business will be shaken by unexpected events, as well as by your competitors making sudden, "out-of-the-blue" advances in the products they offer their customers.

It's also imperative that you have the ability to recognize when the improbable is actually happening to you. We've all seen the horrific images of the Balinese (and now Japanese) tsunami and the unfortunate people standing transfixed on the beach, watching the water slowly get sucked out before it returned as a killer wave. It's easy for us to think, "Run!," but the reality is that when you're standing there, looking at the water, it's much easier to believe "Nothing bad is happening, really, this is fine. Weird, but fine."

You have to be open to seeing the warning signs, the things that are saying, "This is your fifteen-minute warning; you need to run now." Keep your eyes open for the weak signals that let you know something unexpected is coming. Yahoo! ignored the weak signals they were seeing, and they didn't do anything. Don't get lulled by a seemingly slow change and tell yourself that you can handle it, because all of a sudden you could find yourself being washed away.

There is a risk to being number one in your market, like Yahoo!, because it can make you feel you have the right to finally relax; after all, you've gotten to the top of the mountain! The reality is that you are constantly being challenged by the person climbing up behind you. But if you aren't careful, you'll fall into the trap of simply trying to stay ahead of the number-two guy who's trying to catch up with you, rather than focusing on moving forward on your own.

Remember, dealing with jolts isn't just about playing defense, it's also about using them to your advantage, or even creating jolts yourself if they will help you to disrupt your competitors and get ahead of them. Use the questions below as a guide to list possible jolts, and devise ways that you would survive and even profit from them.

The first step toward innovation is shaking loose your assumptions about your organization and preparing for the unexpected jolts that will inevitably come. Apply a critical eye to your own industry. The point isn't to decide that "up equals down" but to shake things up and open your eyes to opportunities you weren't even aware that you were missing. Now, bear in mind that assumptions have an upside, too. We assume certain things because waking up every morning wondering if the basic nuts and bolts of our lives still hold true would waste a whole lot of time and probably cause us some unneeded stress on a daily basis. So it's safe to assume you should follow the basic laws of civilized society. If you run a red light, you'll probably get a ticket. That's a good assumption. There are "good assumptions" within the business world too, but I'm not going to list them for you; it's up to you to run these exercises and do your own filtering to determine which assumptions are beneficial to your work and which are not.

The point is to keep questioning your assumptions *because even good assumptions may go bad.* If you constantly ask yourself questions that challenge you to evaluate what you do, how you do it, and who you do it for, you will automatically be ahead of your competition.

FURTHER QUESTIONS

What situation do you know will never happen to you or your
   business?
What situation is so outside the realm of possibility that there is no
   need to prepare for it on any level?
What would be the effect on your business if it did happen?
How would you respond, and what would you do?

Now, I'm not really asking you to look into a crystal ball and guess the nature of the random jolts that may affect your future. I have zero interest in asking you to consider the possibility of random geological events disrupting your manufacturing or sales. What I am interested in is helping you open your eyes to possibilities that will shake up the "safe" way your organization operates today. There are huge challenges coming in the business world, and you need to accept that your business will be profoundly rattled by jolts that are so unexpected they have no name to describe them.

These jolts are already shaking up the media industry, and I think it's safe to say that similar jolts will reach your industry too, if they haven't already. Recently I did a workshop with one of the big news agencies. Clearly this is an industry in transition. What do you do when the entire premise of your industry is changing? The news agencies have had great success selling content to newspapers for more than 150 years. But the idea of having bureaus scattered all over the world, generating content, is being pushed aside by a hundred million cell phones all linked to Twitter. News agencies are no longer leading the news, but instead are reporting information coming from citizen journalists who are breaking the big stories. Think of Neda, the Iranian protestor whose violent death in the streets of Tehran went global after it was caught on a cell-phone camera.[7] Or Capt. Chesney "Sully" Sullenberger's jaw-dropping save on the Hudson, captured on riverside security cameras.[8] How do you deal with these shifts in how news is gathered and disseminated when the status quo has been a hugely profitable way of doing business since its very inception?

Maybe the future of a news aggregator is some sort of hybrid—one that sources out immediate coverage of events to citizen journalists, but backs it up with seasoned and nuanced commentary, or "slow news" from its established vets. News corporations' continued survival depends on selling their clients on why "slow news" still matters.

The takeaway from this chapter is that you need to learn how to think and observe like an outsider and see the assumptions that others are missing. Ask yourself if your assumptions about you, your work, and your organization are still valid, given constant changes. Ask yourself, "Why am I making these assumptions? What happens if I no longer choose to believe that they apply?" Use the questions in this chapter to find all the areas of your business where you're missing opportunities to make big moves, both for your sake and for that of your organization. Take notes, identify the areas that are going to be most fruitful to investigate, and use this information to set yourself up for the Killer Questions in Part II of the book.

CHAPTER 3

The Corporate Antibodies

So far we've talked about abstract obstacles that can hinder your innovation efforts. However, there is one real flesh-and-blood obstacle that is probably sitting behind a desk somewhere in your organization right now. They may seem harmless, maybe even positive, but they are your biggest obstacle on the path to generating a great idea and turning it into a killer innovation. Learning how to work with, or work *around* them is an invaluable skill on your road to innovation.

The antagonist of the innovator is the corporate antibody. Much as antibodies in our immune system attack and destroy foreign objects that might harm the body, "antibodies" in your organization identify and neutralize forces that threaten to destabilize a company. And in much the same way that antibodies can damage the very thing they seek to protect—for instance when they cause the body to reject a transplanted organ—corporate antibodies can stunt a company's growth when they shut down the fresh ideas and unconventional thinkers it so badly needs.

You've probably dealt with these corporate antibodies many times. They have a thousand reasons why something isn't going to work and

are quick to share them with you the minute you propose a new idea.
Over the years, I've collected a number of the most popular:

Let's shelve that for the time being.
Who is going to do it?
I have something better.
We tried that before.
It won't fit our operation.
Not enough return on investment.
I already thought of that a long time ago.
We can't afford that.
You'll never get approval.
You're on the wrong track.
Don't rock the boat.
The market is not ready yet.
It's not a new concept.
Our customer likes it this way
We are legally obliged to follow these rules.

When I give presentations and hold workshops, I talk about the
corporate antibodies. As I click through the slides revealing the pushback people get when they pitch a new idea, the audience inevitably
starts to laugh. They've either heard them or, worse, said them. Knowing how to recognize and deal with corporate antibodies and these
kinds of statements is a skill you need to master. Why? Because if you
don't know how to deal with this kind of habitual resistance, asking
Killer Questions will be futile. Your ideas—no matter how great they
are—will never get approval.

WHY CORPORATE ANTIBODIES FIGHT BACK

Understanding how to deal with the corporate antibodies is a critical
part of being an innovator. First, look at how the corporate antibody
thinks, and how their point-of-view is different from yours. It's easy

to assume they share your enthusiasm and energy for creating new ideas or pushing for innovation. As an innovator, you believe you can convince others to support your idea based on the logic and obvious benefit, not to mention the conviction with which you present it.

The corporate antibody doesn't see it that way. In some cases, their motives come from a good place. They may have spent decades protecting their "body"—be it a department or the corporation in general—from anything that might threaten it. However, years of fighting back against radical ideas and unfamiliar concepts can train them to push back against any new idea whatsoever. Instead of using "no" judiciously, they use it as their automatic response.

In other cases, the resistance can be motivated by their egos and fears. For example, they may secretly love your idea but turn against it because they wanted to be the person to come up with the game-changer. They may fear experimenting because of a tumultuous marketplace. Perhaps they like the stability of the status quo and simply feel too comfortable to want to go to the trouble of trying to change. Or they might be fatigued after years of trying—and failing—to push through new ideas of their own. No matter the motivations, these corporate antibodies prevent you from building the kind of culture necessary for creating killer innovations.

So how do you deal with this?

OVERCOMING CORPORATE ANTIBODIES

I work in the innovation and technology sector. Many of my coworkers are brilliant individuals, some bordering on genius. Yet many of these men and women have almost no ability to navigate the hurdles between having an idea and getting others to support it. I'm amazed at how few people have the skill to pitch an idea. The pitch is the starting point. It's where you lay out the idea, the rationale behind it, and its potential influence on the organization. If you can't do that effectively and persuasively, getting the corporate antibody to even give your idea a fair shot is lost. Many simply put the facts out there and think,

"Everybody should just get it like I get it." Some people will meander and dither, taking too long to get to the point of the idea. Others are so stubbornly resistant to feedback or compromise that they anger the people they pitch. Still others don't do their research and have no idea how decisions are actually made within their organization.

While all of these shortcomings derail pitches every day, far more damning is a failure to understand the decision makers themselves. Being able to anticipate and react to the conscious and unconscious biases they hold—and sell them an idea—is just as important as being able to create an idea in the first place. Innovation is about doing and making things, so an unsuccessful pitch means no resources, which means no innovation.

Most pushbacks are simply quick, off-the-cuff ways to try to make your idea go away; the antibodies have already made up their minds without really considering it. So what do you do when you're trying to sell a great idea but are getting resistance from the people whose support you need? The first step is nothing. Don't fight—at least, not yet. Don't argue or in any way insinuate that they "don't get it." Instead, take a moment and ask yourself, "OK, why am I getting this pushback?" There are four reasons why a corporate antibody might shoot down your ideas:

1. THE EGO RESPONSE

"Oh, I already thought of that a long time ago."
"Somebody else has already come up with that idea."
"I have something better."

The three examples above are classic ego-driven statements. These people are essentially telling you "Been there, done that." They are brushing you off in a way that suggests that on some level, your idea is threatening the speaker's sense of self, especially if they themselves are a creative or idea person within your organization. Be careful. You may think you are talking about business, but you are actually engaged in a very personal exchange about your respective places in the hierarchy of your organization. In order to get their support, you need to appeal to their ego and satisfy their need for personal validation. Once you've done that, you can do the necessary work to satisfy them that the idea makes business sense as well.

When you're dealing with a corporate antibody who is fueled by ego, the most important thing to do is show you're not challenging them. If they give you feedback, look at it as a possible opportunity for getting further support from them. Put their suggestions to work in your idea and your pitch, and acknowledge that it came from them. Take a moment to recognize them and their contribution, both in writing and when you deliver your revised pitch. Why do you want to do this? Because you've now given them a sense of ownership in the idea. No matter what their original doubts and hesitations, they are going to be more inclined to support your idea now.

2. THE FATIGUED RESPONSE

"You'll never get approval."
"We tried that before."
"Who's going to do it?"
"It won't fit our operation."

Sometimes ego isn't the problem. A big issue with corporate antibodies is fatigue. Perhaps their nature is to support new ideas with enthusiasm and energy, but the corporate culture is conservative to the point where they can't get those ideas executed. When they hear your pitch, their inner voice says, "I've pitched a dozen ideas in the last five years to management and all of them got blown out of the water; none of them got approved." They are so burned out that they only half listen to new ideas, assuming they've heard it all and tried it all before. They simply can't deal with the thought of going through the process again.

Remember that you're the person who wants something, so, fairly or unfairly, you have to go more than halfway. How should you recraft your idea to make an executive feel excited about taking on your idea and promoting it? Can you rework your idea so you're asking them to take little steps rather than asking for a big commitment up front? Remember, step outside of yourself and hear your pitch with their ears. The fatigued corporate antibody feels like he's heard everything you have to say many times before. As you describe your idea, his biases automatically kick in, and they draw connections between your new concept and old ideas that didn't work. They zero in on one of these perceived links and start to tune out everything else. Your job now is to draw their biases out, understand what old experiences they remember, and figure out a way to demonstrate that these things aren't applicable to your new concept. Keep the dialogue going. Ask questions, and get them engaged in your ideas by asking for their opinions. Remember that the information they share is valuable; they've witnessed many ideas and innovations getting shot down. They understand what went wrong, and how you can prevent the same thing happening now. Try to listen more than you talk, and hold off on responding until they've finished. Every question you can ask draws the corporate antibody closer to supporting you, because, whether they realize it or not, they are slowly becoming invested in your idea.

If you can keep the momentum going, at some point you'll see an opportunity for a direct question about the viability of your idea. Take it; find a way to demonstrate that your idea will not play out their worst fears about repeating past experiences. All you need is one acknowledgment that there is an opportunity that didn't exist before to turn it around.

3. THE NO-RISK RESPONSE

"Not enough return on investment."
"We can't afford that."

There's no risk in saying no; there's a risk in saying yes. When you hear automatic responses like this, you're dealing with a corporate antibody who understands that doing nothing might not advance their career or their standing in the company, but it avoids any downside risk. The "no-risk" corporate antibody will often tie these statements together, so you'll hear "We can't afford to risk R&D on an idea that won't give us a sufficient return on investment."

"No-risk" is essentially stagnancy, and it can be incredibly hard to work around. Try to hear your pitch from their perspective. The "no-risk" antibody is willing to stall the companies' evolution rather than take a chance by committing dollars to a new idea. You may think you've got a foolproof strategy, but they might be hearing "Hey, take this big leap: Get me ten million dollars and I'll promise this thing is going to be fantastic, trust me." The most effective way to get them to support you is to demonstrate that there is less risk than they think. Use the gated funding model we will be discussing in chapter 5 and make it clear that supporting the first stage of your idea will be low-risk, low-cost, and does not commit them to moving on to a bigger investment. Think of the "no-risk" antibody as a commitment-phobe; let him know that he can give up on the idea whenever he wants, and he is more likely to stay interested in it. Figure out how you get people comfortable with risk. Rather than making it a one-shot "big-bang" commitment, figure out how you can chop your concept down into smaller steps. Asking for a few thousand dollars to prove that the customer really needs the product is going to get a yes faster than asking for the full budget (and the attendant risk) all at once.

There is also a more dramatic way to deal with a "no-risk" antibody. One of the classic stories of innovation at HP was when David Packard awarded Chuck House the Medal of Defiance for deliberately defying Dave's orders and forcing through an idea he had about a next-generation oscilloscope.[1] David Packard himself ordered the idea killed. When the product turned out to be highly successful, David Packard admitted he was wrong and presented Chuck an award "in recognition of extraordinary contempt and defiance, beyond the normal call of engineering duty."[2]

This speaks to a subtle truth about innovation. Chuck believed in his invention, but he couldn't get any support for it. The lack of support wasn't because of the cost of his invention, it was more a fundamental belief on the part of management that the product wasn't worth pursuing. Chuck believed that if he got his oscilloscope into the catalogue, it would sell. Turns out he was correct, and the oscilloscope ended up selling 17,000 units instead of the predicted 31.[3] Beyond its success, the core product was modified and used by NASA to enable the world to watch Neil Armstrong walk on the moon. Without Chuck's defiance, the world would only have listened to "One small step for a man, one giant leap for mankind" on the radio rather than watching the landing as it happened.[4]

Sometimes there is no other way around a "no-risk" corporate antibody than a slightly cunning reinterpretation of the rules, or selective hearing when you're told no. I'm not advocating lying, deceit, or anything of that nature; rather, you need to understand that within most organizations you'll find far more people who feel empowered to say no than people who feel they are empowered to say yes. So you are always more likely to hear a no than its positive counterpart. Don't lie, but don't always wait for permission, either. If you truly believe in an idea, and you're willing to take a risk, put your plan in motion. There are multiple paths to your objective. If you can't get direct approval, then sometimes avoiding explicit disapproval is almost as good. You can always ask for forgiveness later.

4. THE COMFORT RESPONSE

"We've always done it this way."
"Our customer likes it this way."
"Don't rock the boat."

What constitutes success? Do you need a specific kind of victory in order to feel like you succeeded, or can you redefine success over the years to reflect the realities of your business? When corporate antibodies tell you that change isn't desirable or feasible, they may be locked in some very outdated thinking about what success looks like. It's up to you to find ways to convince them that what constitutes success may well have changed.

Look at how the treatment of HIV has evolved. Twenty years ago, most HIV patients had two potential outcomes: die now or die in the very near future. Success in the battle against AIDS was narrowly defined as finding a cure. Now, twenty-six years later, the HIV drug cocktails have allowed doctors, researchers, and patients to redefine what success means. It has evolved from finding a cure to giving AIDS patients a similar quality of life, and lifespan, as they would have enjoyed had they not become infected.[5] So, you need to be aware that the goalposts can move, for both good and bad reasons. Be aware that there are two negative results of the comfort response: You can either become so ingrained in your answer that you never want to let go, or so unfocused and disorganized that you'll chase any possible answer. If you're getting feedback that your business has already identified clear definitions of success and that your project does not fall within those parameters, then you need to either move your goalposts or persuade them to move theirs.

Consider this example from the world of fashion. In the 1990s, Gucci designer Tom Ford redefined what a fashion show was, and how a fashion designer communicated with the mass audience who would eventually be buying his products.[6] He anticipated how the previously "members only" fashion world was going mainstream, and created decadent runway shows and boldly sexual advertising that spoke directly to the end consumer. In the mid-'90s, turning a somewhat dusty fashion house into a global megabrand was success, and the maximum exposure equated to maximum sales.[7]

Of course, you can't assume that things will stay the same in any industry. When Ford returned to fashion in 2010 after a hiatus, he asked the same question: "How do I keep people really, really wanting this?" but came up with totally different answer. During his tenure at Gucci, he changed the fundamental assumption of success by challenging fashion's exclusivity. He created an assumption that fashion was instantaneously accessible. Anyone who wanted to see or experience high fashion could. That definition of success ultimately eroded *any* sense of exclusivity, however. Ford's first fashion show under his own name was a bold statement about making fashion exclusive again. His presentation had 100 invited guests, no cameras or bloggers allowed, and celebrities like Beyoncé modeling. Ford flipped the switch and completely reversed the goalposts. Rather than courting publicity and seeking maximum exposure, he shunned it. By minimizing access, he maximized impact. This paid off in early spring 2011, when every major fashion magazine ran editorials and interviews about him and his collection.[8]

The point is that you need to understand that while your core mission may stay the same, the way you define success in achieving it may change. In Tom Ford's case, he considered how to get to his end customer, the woman who was really buying his clothes. The first wave meant selling to buyers, the second meant opening up the experience to include everybody who wanted to be part of it. And the third was realizing that the definitions of success had to change, and that to reclaim a sense of luxury he had to exclude just about everybody. All these tactics are in pursuit of the same goal: a luxurious, in-demand brand with high status recognition and sales to match. The approaches are simply different definitions of success when it comes to building a brand and customer loyalty.

||||||||||||

You may think corporate antibodies are being needlessly conservative, but they believe they are keeping the company safe. This is especially true when you're standing on the other side of the desk from an antibody, and they've just shot down your idea. The reality is that the antibodies believe that they are working in the best interests of their employer and their customers. They believe that they are serving as gatekeepers, and are the last line of defense against people or ideas that might damage the organization. To get them on your side, you need to convince them that you aren't a threat and that your idea is actually aligned with and complementary to their ideals. When they start to see your idea as a "good change" with a clear path to success, rather than a "bad change" or an experiment, then you stand a chance of winning them over.

FIGHT OR FLIGHT

I have a very simple reason for being passionate about pushing back against corporate antibodies. Nearly all great ideas require nerve, vision, and guts to get in motion. The corporate antibody is the first of many hurdles that you'll need to push your idea past. If you can't develop the skills to work around your in-house adversaries, you are going to struggle to ever get your ideas and innovations off of the ground. Even if you are unable to get their support for your idea, try to look at your interactions with them as valuable learning experiences. If you are unable to get them on board and supportive, figure out why. Break down your interactions, figure out where the mistakes were made in the past, and decide how you will do things differently in the future, both with corporate antibodies and the organization as a whole.

If you find yourself turning down a great idea because you believe that "it's been done before" or "customers will never accept it," then there's a good chance that someone else will be willing to take the risk. In 1976, Steve Wozniak, later of Apple Computers, was working at HP.[9] In March of that year, he built the first truly personal computer. He thought he was onto a pretty good idea. Wozniak approached his then manager and said he thought his creation had potential and HP should really take this to market. When he was turned down, he left HP, and he and Steve Jobs formed their own company and offered the computer for sale as a DIY kit. They called it the Apple 1.[10] You know how that story turns out.

If an idea doesn't fit into the context of what a person knows, understands, and believes in, it's easy to see it as folly. Years later, the manager who declined to take that first personal computer to market,

Dave Cochran, was gracious enough to do an interview with me for my podcast. When I brought up the story, Cochran was quiet for a second and said, "Yeah, I looked at him and I said, 'Who would want a personal computer?'" He paused for a second and added, "Who knew?"

When you're looking at the corporate antibodies in your organization and coming up with strategies for getting around their objections, be aware of how their fears and "walls" might be affecting the overall health of your company. Most organizations have some sort of long-range, three-to-five-year plan in place. This isn't a bad thing; the problem arises when the antibodies insist that, come hell or high water, they're sticking to the plan, whether it turns out to be a good one or not.

Other organizations get a management team in place that's focused on benchmarking to their peers. Rather than assess potential innovations on their individual merits, they look at them simply as equalizers: "Will this new product get us on par with our competitors?" Corporate antibodies have the classic "tall poppy" syndrome. They don't want to try to rise above the field of their competitors. They fear that standing out in the crowd makes them conspicuous, more vulnerable to attack. And because a tall poppy gets cut down out of the field of flowers, they fear that drawing attention to themselves will be a negative, rather than a positive, situation.

Be aware of the antibodies' fears; but also keep in mind your own needs. If you are constantly being shut down by antibodies, and your attempts to circumvent them and push your ideas through are continually thwarted, you may have to accept that they are there to stay. In that case, you need to make a judgment call: Is it better for you to be continually held back by these people, or do you make a bold move to an organization that will support your ideas?

PART II:

ASKING YOUR WAY TO BREAKTHROUGH INNOVATIONS

CHAPTER 4

Innovate or Die

As I mentioned earlier, twelve years ago I semi-retired. I'd had some early success, and I realized my kids were about to take off for college. If I ever wanted to actually spend some time with my family, it was now or never. At that time, my wife and I owned a small horse farm in Virginia. When I wasn't busy with the horses, I sat on a few boards, offered some advice to start-ups, and even did a little angel investing. As you can imagine, the idea of a quiet country life, surrounded by my family and our horses, was enticing after twenty years of hard work and constant travel.

The thing about retiring at an early age is that it's great for the first few months, but then you start to wonder what's going on back in the "real world." I was able to retire—however temporarily it turned out to be—because I had been successful at generating ideas and translating them into market-leading innovations. I was challenged by friends and business associates to see if there was a way to turn my approach toward creating ideas into a teachable program, something that I could share with the broader business community as well as my innovation clients.

One of the challenges with generating ideas (ideation) is bringing some order to what can feel like a very chaotic process. Ideation can often feel disorganized; there are multiple sources of ideas, and so many possibilities that generating, sorting, and organizing them can start to feel overwhelming. Everyone has an idea, and these ideas can sometimes seem to be in direct conflict with one another.

After many months of hard work, I came up with a system that brought order and strategy to this potentially chaotic process of ideation. The system is broken down into two sections: the Killer Questions, and FIRE—a methodology for using the questions that I'll get to in a minute. The Killer Questions section is organized into three chapters, Who, What, and How (chapters 6, 7, and 8 respectively), and most of these questions come with examples that illustrate companies that have used Killer Questions to their advantage, or ignored them to their peril. At times you will be prompted to ask, "Which Killer Question would have generated this idea?" Each question also comes with a set of three or four Sparking Points. These are designed to replicate the experience of being challenged in a Killer Innovation Workshop to think beyond the obvious.

I think you will find parallels between your organization and the companies I profiled and therefore have some ideas for questions that jump out, but I'd suggest reading through all three Killer Question chapters before you attempt to organize an innovation workshop of your own. You may also find that an unlikely question jumps out at you just because of something that is happening at the moment within your organization. It's important to work through all three areas, Who, What, and How, even if you believe that you and your company don't need help in one or more of them. At the end of the book, you'll find a workshop chapter, which will give you a more detailed breakdown of how to run an innovation workshop using the questions.

||||||||||||

The Killer Questions and the FIRE method are your road map to remaking yourself as a "creative." I firmly believe that we are in the early stages of a new economy, one where the most valuable talent you can bring to the table is being an "idea person." Knowledge is quickly becoming a commodity (think of the thousands of highly capable educational institutions springing up in India, China, and other areas of the world), and simply being well educated is no longer as valuable as it used to be. In order to keep ahead, you need to be able to access and use your creative ability to help your organization address its challenges, continuously coming up with new ideas. This applies even if you've always assumed you aren't creative.

People imagine that ideas come easily to those blessed with creative powers. This is nonsense. Creativity is hard work. Anyone who works in a creative field such as art, architecture, or fashion knows that it takes a hundred scrunched-up, tossed-behind-the-desk rejected sketches to come up with one good one. The same happens when you create ideas for your business or products. Rather than waiting for that "magic moment," take what you are learning from this book, practice it, and then use it. The result is that you will have officially rebranded yourself as a "creative," and you will therefore think like one—which means being fearless about generating ideas and putting them down on paper.

CHAPTER 5

The FIRE Method

Before we dive into the questions, I want to cover some critically important ground. You need to understand how the use of questions fits into the overall methodology of innovation. My objective in creating an approach to innovation was to develop a simple structure that can (1) be applied to *any size business*, (2) be flexible enough to deal with the challenge of coming up with ideas, and (3) help identify the most important ones to work on and improve the chances of translating the ideas into successful killer innovations. The methodology is built around FIRE.

The FIRE acronym stands for Focus, Ideation, Ranking, and Execution. It is a four-part system that uses questions to give structure to the process of choosing where to focus your ideation efforts, improving the quantity and quality of ideas, ranking the ideas so that you know which ones to work on, and then executing them.

FIRE turns the often frustratingly open-ended and unguided work we all have experienced in the past into a workable protocol capable of being carried out. This method will make you confident that the idea you are executing is the very strongest one possible.

WHY FIRE WORKS

The main challenges that all organizations face are what I call the innovation gap and the innovation delay. The innovation gap is the difference between the need for really great ideas and the actual supply of them. All organizations can use a supply of more and better ideas. The Focus, Ideation, and Ranking stages of FIRE address the innovation gap by giving you a system that improves the quantity and quality of ideas. The innovation delay refers to how long it takes you to go from selecting an idea for execution to getting a product to market. To address the delay, the Execution stage of FIRE gives you tools to improve the success rate of turning your ideas into killer innovations.

Both the gap and the delay can be traced back to the corporate antibodies and their assumptions about how your organization should operate, the ideas that will work for it, and who your customers are. Now, the gap is an easy concept to understand because most people acknowledge that a constant flow of better ideas is required to stay ahead of the game. Same with the delay; most businesspeople have had the experience of bringing a good product to market too late, so that makes sense too. The problem isn't so much getting people to see the gap and the delay as it is giving them the confidence that there is a way around them.

THE FOUR ELEMENTS OF FIRE

FOCUS

Identify the areas (e.g., customers, products, etc.) where you want/need to innovate.

IDEATION

Generate great ideas by asking Killer Questions.

RANKING

Rank your ideas using five simple questions to identify the best.

EXECUTION

Turn your best idea into a Killer Innovation through a question-based stage-gate process.

Focus

The first stage of FIRE, Focus, is about doing a thorough but organized search, so you don't inadvertently ignore a critical area of discovery. Successful innovation is the translation of ideas into something, such as a product, that is real. If you are focused in your approach, you will be able to decide if there is an idea worth pursuing with much less stress than if you are scattershot in your approach. When I was twenty-eight years old, I was given my first big opportunity to prove myself at Thumbscan, a company that did pioneering work in fingerprint biometric security. Thumbscan was thinking about acquiring a company called Gordian Systems.[1] Gordian had one product: a token security device that was quite popular in the government but didn't have any other customers. Despite the viability of the product, they weren't making enough money, and they looked set to go out of business. I was asked to go look at Gordian and see if I could come up with an idea for a product that would justify Thumbscan acquiring the company.[2]

The first thing I noticed was that Gordian was highly focused on catering to their government contracts, to the extent that they couldn't think beyond selling one product to one customer. Their rules and assumptions were so locked into "This is what we do," they literally couldn't consider doing anything differently. The first thing I thought when I met with the Gordian team members was "Why aren't they thinking more broadly?" I couldn't understand why they weren't asking, "Are there other customers who could benefit from what we've developed?" "What do they need, and how would we develop and support it?" "What are the new issues in corporate PC security going to be?" They had one customer who loved what they did, but it didn't make big enough orders to support the entire company. Yet they were so focused on this customer that they were missing the other customers and products that they could have developed.

Of course, part of my approach was expediency; I'd been given a very small window of time to come up with something that justified acquiring the assets. I didn't have the time to sit in a room for days, coming up with a compelling idea; I needed a solid product concept within the next day or so. Rather than just sitting down and waiting for a magic idea to come up, I went through and did a methodical search, point-by-point. Over the course of one day, I looked at three areas of Focus: (1) Who are the potential new customers we could we target? (2) What would we have to build to appeal to them? And (3) How would we do it? What I wanted to find out was simple: "Could we come up with a unique product?" At the end of the twenty-four hours, I had the beginnings of an idea called PC Boot. PC Boot took Gordian Systems' existing technology and applied it to a whole new audience— the burgeoning business PC market.

The point here is that the first step to successful ideation is to bring focus to the areas with the greatest opportunity. Rather than waiting for serendipity to happen, you are concentrating on the areas where innovation could have the biggest effect on your organization. Focus is structured to make sure you've looked carefully at every area of your business, without missing any area of opportunity.

Think of an astronomer searching the sky for new stars. They will study very small areas of the sky, very intently. When they have observed everything there is to see, they move on to the next small area. Focus is not about limiting the search, but instead using a systematic approach to make sure all the relevant areas are covered. There are three areas that any innovation effort needs to look at in order to cover all their bases:

- **Who** is the person or organization that you sell your product or service to (i.e., your customer)?
- **What** is the product or service you deliver to the customer?
- **How** does your organization create, deliver, and support the product (what) to the customer (who)?

In my experience, most organizations focus on the customer (who) and the product (what). They tend to ignore everything else the organization does in order to function (how). You will automatically be miles ahead of your competitors simply by looking at all of these areas rather than limiting yourself to just one of them.

I would suggest you go through them one at a time and try not to tackle all of them at once. However, it is important that you cover all three areas eventually, otherwise you will leave yourself open to potential blind spots. Focus should be a never-ending process of cycling through all three areas, ensuring you are on top of the continual changes and evolutions in your industry.

If you're not sure which area is the most relevant to your needs, just pick one. You'll be going through them all eventually.

Ideation

The Killer Questions are used in the Ideation phase of FIRE. The point of the Killer Questions is to keep you focused on a specific facet of your organization, your customer, your product, or your operations, but at the same time keep your search for ideas expansive within that area. The Killer Questions will help you to look at problems from perspectives you hadn't previously considered and will keep you open to seeing potential answers that fall outside of your existing assumptions about how and why you do things the way you do.

It is important to realize that ideas can come from unexpected places. Don't make the mistake of assuming that ideas come from a certain person or department within your organization. Instead, keep your eyes open to the possibility that a great idea can come from a seemingly random place. Use the questions, and be open to being surprised by the answers.

Six or seven years ago I took part in a brainstorming session to come up with ideas for a video about future uses for technology. We went through a few concepts, asking, "What will five years in the future look like?" One of the ideas we all liked was exploring how technology in the home might be integrated with mobile technology in the future. I paused and said, "That triggers something," and I told the group about an evening earlier that year.

It was a point in time when I was traveling back and forth between Virginia and California on a weekly basis. On one of these trips, I had arrived home late on a Friday. My oldest daughter, Tara, was home from college. We stayed up and chatted before I crashed for the evening. That night I was asleep for a few hours when I heard footsteps on the tin roof of our house. I went out the back door, dressed only in my boxers, and shined the flashlight on the roof. I was amazed to see a boy tapping on Tara's window. I shouted up at him, "What are you doing up there?" When he saw me, he turned white, but he managed to squeak out, "Uh, Mr. McKinney, I need to talk to Tara." Turns out Tara had broken up with him that day, and he was desperate to try to talk her out of her decision.

In the meantime, the neighbors had seen the boy's car parked on the street and had called the local police. The six-foot-four state trooper who got out of the car thought the whole thing was hysterical. At least until I told him, "When your kids start dating, you are going to remember this night!"

I told this story, then we moved on to other subjects and I forgot about it. But the creative team behind the video project didn't. A few months later, they screened the videos for us and, to my shock, one of the videos was about a remote home-security-monitoring device based on the "Boy on the Roof" story. Ideas come from unexpected places; you may have great ones hidden in your own experiences, stories, and observations, but sometimes it can take another pair of eyes and ears to recognize their potential value.

So, when you're in the Ideation phase, it's critical to be open to the possibility that a great idea will come from a seemingly random place. Don't discount an idea simply because it isn't what you expected or it's not coming from the person or place you assumed it would come from.

Ranking

Once you've generated your ideas, the next step is to figure out which ideas have the potential to become innovations. So, how do you decide which ideas to work on? The typical innovation process leaves that decision to the senior-level managers, which seems like a logical choice. They're senior, so they should have the wisdom to make the best choices, right? Unfortunately, they often aren't involved in the process of creating and selecting the best ideas. Because of this, the ideas they like may well be heavily influenced by their personal preferences and biases. If this is the case, the chance of the ideas selected becoming killer innovations will be low. A properly defined ranking system, on the other hand, helps people to set aside their biases and look at ideas from a bigger-picture perspective.

Many believe that the ranking process for selecting the best ideas must be some kind of complex set of analytics. It is not. I've developed a very simple and elegant process. The ranking system uses questions to determine which ideas not only will have significant results but are also aligned with your core capabilities and expertise. It's based on having the team score five questions for every idea generated in the workshop. The final scores rank your ideas from best to worst, which allows you to clearly see which ones you should pursue further. You'll see the full breakdown in chapter 9, but for now it's simply important to remember that you must be confident that you can identify the best ideas and ultimately select the idea most worthy of execution.

One of the most interesting aspects of developing the ranking process was realizing how careful we needed to be to weed out bias and influence in the voting phase. I quickly found that we'd get completely different results when people knew their vote was anonymous versus when they were voting in a public forum with a bunch of senior execs in the room. I've been thrown out of workshops by my own team leaders because of the concern that "people will want to make Phil happy." I have to constantly be on guard not to have that kind of an influence. Originally, I had a dot system that was quick to use and simple to tally. The people in the workshop had red, green, and yellow dots that were respectively worth one, two, and three points. At the end of a workshop, participants walked up and put their dots on the ideas they liked. Seems simple, right? Unfortunately I quickly realized that people were waiting to see what the alpha-dog executive voted for, then immediately rallied behind his or her votes. The votes were aggregated and lost any usefulness because they essentially reflected only one person's opinion. Anonymity significantly changes the group dynamics, so it's critical to keep people unaware of how the other participants are voting.

Execution

My motto throughout my career has been "Ideas without execution are a hobby, and I'm not in the hobby business." Execution is a risk; it requires commitment, money, and manpower; but there's no point going through the process of ideation if you're not going to do anything with the end result. In the end, successful execution is a balance between pushing your organization to take a risk and pressing your case so hard that you scare the corporate antibodies into retreat. My execution strategy is to manage risk in the execution process, starting each innovation so that it makes it to the execution stage in a small and scrappy way. The execution phase makes the corporate antibodies nervous, so in order to get their support, you're going to need to take the emotion and fear out of the process.

The execution portion of FIRE uses a "gated funding" system to ensure that the good ideas get a chance to prove themselves while guaranteeing that the organization is not overexposed to risk in the event that an idea doesn't work.

THE GATED FUNDING MODEL

The gated funding model (or stage-gate model) means that an idea has to pass through a set of predetermined goals, or "gates," to progress toward becoming an actual product. The gated funding model limits the risk by forcing ideas to meet predetermined standards. If an idea passes a gate, it gets additional resources (people, budget, etc.) and a new set of goals that the team will need to achieve to move on to the next gate.

There are four gates: market validation, customer validation, limited launch, and global launch. At each gate, there are a series of questions/metrics that need to be answered before an idea is approved for additional resources. For instance, a team might have to commit to talking to 100 potential customers to verify there is consumer interest for a product.

In addition to the questions/metrics, each gate comes with a timeframe in which progress must be made. A project shouldn't be allowed to limp along forever. The team needs to realize that they have a certain amount of time to answer the questions at each gate. If they are exceeding the specified time frame, then you need to start asking "What's taking so long?"

Ideas will be narrowed down as they flow through the gated funding model as described here:

Market Validation: All Ranked Ideas
Customer Validation: ~50% of ideas from Gate 1
Limited Launch: ~50% of ideas from Gate 2
Global Launch: ~50% of ideas from Gate 3

As a real-world example, my team looks to fund ~20 ideas into the market-validation phase. The result is that ~12 make it into customer

THE FOUR GATES

Market Validation

This gate requires your team to prove that there is a problem—in other words, that there is a customer group out there who will want to purchase what you are proposing. Your team needs to get out there and verify firsthand that there is a market for an idea. Don't rely on existing research and don't accept third-party studies as evidence you should proceed.

Customer Validation

This gate helps you evaluate whether you can create a solution to the problem. Put something in front of customers, regardless of whether it's a Rube Goldberg mockup of an eventual product, a video, or a sample—anything that allows the customer to see, feel, and experience the idea.

Are your potential customers willing to pay for your idea? Is the revenue and margin matching up to the overall business model? This is the key gate to understanding whether this idea satisfies the needs of the customer *and* has the potential to meet the revenue and margin requirements to make it a viable business.

Limited Launch

Build and sell the product to real customers in a limited market or trial. One of the key measurements for success in this phase is your customer reaction now that they are actually parting with cash for your product or service. You want to determine if you can get your sales teams excited about it, and that they are confident that they can make sales.

Determine what constitutes success in this category, and whether you will generate sufficient volume. Are customers willing to pay for it, and is the revenue and margin potential matching up with the business model? Can the organization elevate this idea into a global launch?

Global Launch

This is it. The factories are geared up, and there's no going back. The final step is to integrate the idea into your overall business. This sounds much easier than it is in real life. The approach that has worked for me is to have a gradual handoff that starts to occur with the customer validation gate. At that point, you want the eventual owners of the product to be engaged and starting to take emotional ownership of the idea and its execution. As the idea progresses, that team takes on more and more of the execution responsibility to the point where you reach global launch and they fully own it.

validation. For limited launch, we have 5 or 6 at any one time, with the net result being that we launch 2 to 3 products per year.

This approach works both because it sets limits on risk but also because it forces the people involved in implementing an idea to justify the idea at each gate by meeting a set of defined criteria (e.g., Will customers buy this product?).

One of the keys I've found to successful execution is constraint-based innovation. It is exactly what it sounds like. When I'm in the execution phase of the innovation process and assigning teams to various ideas, I'll ask them, "How long will it take for you to create the product?" Whatever answer they give me, for example, "Oh, it'll be twenty-four months," I'll counter with less time, less money, or less manpower. When I tell them that we really need to figure out how to get the product pulled together in twelve months, they push back but eventually go off and try to figure out how.

I've found over the years that if you give a team the full time that they ask for, or the full budget that they want, or the full number of people that they need, those teams never execute anything of significance. But if you give them less, make things a little more challenging, they'll push themselves. When they have some form of constraint, it forces them to have to think in a unique way. Think of the Apollo 13 mission and how constraint aided them in coming up with a highly creative solution, very quickly. When they come in with a standard approach, they unconsciously revert to the way "that has worked before." This is exactly the opposite of what I want them to do. If, on the other hand, the parameters are changed and they are forced to move fast, they will have to find a new way to meet the objective, since the old way won't work. In the end, you get results.

Bear in mind that you won't necessarily have one sure-fire great idea coming out of a workshop; that's not actually the point of the Ideation or the Ranking exercises. What Ideation and Ranking will give you is the best possible selection of ideas to pursue, arranged in order of quality and applicability. You most likely will find that the ideas that typically get implemented are not identical to the ideas that come out of the workshop. So, at each of the four gates, even in the execution phase, you're still looking at questions like: "How do I take this idea and make it bigger?" "How do I make it better?" "How do I make it have more influence?" "How do I make it have even more of a differentiator?" "How do I make it stand out?" Remember that ideas can still evolve, even late in the game in the execution phase.

WHY YOU NEED A SYSTEM

So, what happens if you don't use a system like FIRE to innovate and execute the strongest ideas? One of the biggest dangers of not having a way to identify and execute the best ideas is that weak ideas get selected and the results are disappointing. When this happens, management loses confidence that the organization has the ability to come up with killer ideas and then turns to outsiders or acquisitions to fill the gap.

Another potential pitfall is that management will stick with an idea long after it should have been killed. It's human nature to get emotionally invested in the things you create, but this emotion can be destructive, as it encourages you to march blindly on, without questioning whether what you are doing can actually become a killer innovation. The execution phase of FIRE forces you to ask if your idea really achieves its objectives. It creates checks and balances so that everyone involved continually asks, "Why are we doing the project? Is this the best idea?"

A great example of what happens when a pet project gets selected happened in England in the late '90s.

In the run-up to the millennium, the then-ruling Tory Party decided they needed to make a statement of some sort to celebrate such an epochal event.[3] Land, formerly the site of a demolished gasworks in the southeast Docklands, was assigned. A budget, much of it funded by the new National Lottery, allocated. The design, essentially a huge dome-like tent, was drawn up. There was a vague idea that the Dome would eventually be part of a larger event, such as the Festival of Britain. The problem was that nobody had much of an idea of what the Dome would actually contain. Sure, it would be visually dramatic when viewed from above or from a distance, but being pleasant to look at didn't justify its billion-pound-plus eventual price tag and symbolic gravitas.[4] Nobody took the time to define the Who or What of the project's focus.

The Dome was already flailing when the Tories were ushered out of power in 1997 and replaced by Labour and its "Cool Britannia" philosophy.[5] The UK's economy was growing and its cultural power was at its apex, with bands like Oasis and the Spice Girls waving the Union Jack around the world. So you can't really blame the new Labour government for feeling a sense of confidence about the Dome. They pushed on with the project, despite grumbles that "governments shouldn't try to run tourist attractions."[6] The Dome opened on New Year's Eve, 1999. Ticketing problems meant that some VIP guests were waiting in lines to enter the structure when midnight struck. Later, when blame started to be assigned, the head of the Dome project insinuated that every decision had been made by a committee, even selecting the fabric trim for the entertainers' acrobatic costumes.[7] The exhibits eventually chosen to reside within the Dome certainly reflected this design-by-consensus. They were sponsored by various large corporations and were generally viewed as underwhelming at best. Attendance never reached the projected numbers, and the Dome closed for business on December 30, 2000—the day before the new millennium actually started.

I wonder if anyone ever sat down and asked a few questions about the purpose of what they were doing and whether it would meet the needs of their "Who"—the British people. Some of the questions I'd have wanted to ask would have been:

- Does your *What* have any value to the customers?
- Has anyone put real thought into whether it can generate tax revenue, or contribute in some way versus being a drain on the UK's economy?
- Do you really have the ability to pull it off; do you have the *How* infrastructure and skills to make this work?
- Has anyone considered the kill/pause option? Or is the Dome still proceeding because of blind faith and an unwillingness to admit error?

Bottom line: There is no point in just "doing something" because you can. You can throw all the money, time, and manpower you want at a concept. If there is no reason or thought behind why you are doing it and what you hope to accomplish, you will end up with your own version of what Prince Charles described as looking like a monstrous jelly pudding.[8]

Think about the Dome the next time you are working on some random idea that the boss came up with. Ideas for ideas' sake are worthless. The objective is to have a process that ensures you identify the best ideas that will turn into killer innovations. I doubt the Dome would have made it through the FIRE system, and it's a great example of why you need such a system in place.

||||||||||||||

We'll return to the FIRE method in chapter 9, but for now, read the Who, What, and How Killer Questions in chapters 6, 7, and 8. Assuming you need to generate some great ideas for your company, these questions should help you push yourself, and your team, to come up with a robust list of fresh possibilities to rank later.

So if you haven't already started taking notes, grab a notebook and a pen. Jot down anything that comes to mind as you read through the Questions. I'm a big fan of writing in the margins and generally making a mess of my books. These exercises are interactive, so begin now. Don't let a thought go without noting it down. You never know where these random ideas will lead.

Getting to Know Your Who

A couple of years ago, my kids gave my ninety-three-year-old grandma a digital picture frame for Christmas. It contained several hundred photos that they had painstakingly selected, organized, and then downloaded onto it. Every minute or so, a new image of the kids living their lives would appear—exactly the kind of thing any grandmother would love, right? She happily plugged it in and set it on a side table next to her armchair. The next time I visited my grandma, I glanced at the frame and noticed the picture wasn't changing. Finally, I had to get up and see what was going on. Turns out there was nothing wrong with the frame. Instead, my grandma had unplugged it and stuck a regular print photo in front of the high-resolution screen. When I asked her why, she said that she was worried about the cost of running the gadget. And, she added, it might short out and catch fire in the middle of the night. The next day, my daughter Tara uploaded a picture of the frame onto Facebook. Underneath it, she wrote, "Grandma's Digital Picture Frame: FAIL."

Grandma's picture frame is a funny family story, but it's also a great example of a basic truth in innovation. You can't always assume you know *who* your customers are, or why they might want, or reject, what you're offering them. You don't know what their motivations are, or what they really want. As you'll see in this chapter, understanding your customer depends on two things: knowing the people whose needs you could fill, and getting a better grasp on the criteria they use to choose a product. Once you know the former, you can tailor your actions to the latter. Then you're on your way to truly understanding how to best serve your customers.

My grandma grew up in the Depression. She never forgot what that era was like, specifically the struggle to survive and the intense fear of poverty. She had seen and heard of families who were ruined over small debts, and as a child she had vowed to never be in that position. Grandma saw this picture frame from an entirely different point of view than my kids and I did. For us, it was a whimsical, fun gift with no possible downside. To her, it was something whose use had to be carefully weighed against the possible risks it presented. She fretted over the perceived cost and safety issues of the frame, to the point that she took no pleasure in the hundreds of photographs it contained. I told her that the monthly cost to run it was roughly ten cents, and that there was no chance of her house burning down, but no dice. The digital picture frame didn't meet any of my grandma's unspoken needs and wants. Lesson learned.

|||||||||||||

The point of this chapter is simple: All your work, all your ideas, all your devotion and sacrifice mean nothing if you're not confident of whom you are doing it for or why. In order to succeed—whether you are developing a new product, service, or process—you must understand the needs, wants, and sometimes fears of the person you are targeting.

Why is this so hard to actually do? In a way, it's all about you, and your over-confidence in your expertise, experience, and education. These things define your perception of the world. Eventually, you no longer realize that your broadest assumptions about the world come from the narrowest of perspectives—your own. You might be tempted to believe that you can know your customer without having actually done the legwork of going out and discovering just who they are. However, it is dangerous to assume (perhaps because of demographics, or perhaps because you started your company for people just like you) that they share your values, dreams, and beliefs.

This common mistake was beautifully illustrated a few years ago at a meeting with a group of engineers, marketing people, and management at a Silicon Valley company. At regular sessions like this one, teams review ideas for future concepts. This is the time to pitch your best idea and to get management's green light to move forward. In this particular meeting, one of the team members got up to present his take on a new concept. The CTO watched, fascinated, as he ran through the features he felt would make it a success. His ideas were innovative, yet he couldn't grasp why a customer would want some, if not most, of the features. Instead of adding value, they added complexity. In the CTO's opinion, the eventual owner of this product was going to be frustrated, not excited. When the CTO inquired about which customers were asking for the specific features, the engineer responded that he didn't know; he hadn't talked with customers. He'd added the features because *he* wanted them. The result was a set of features designed for engineers rather than an everyday customer.

I see examples of this kind of backward thinking all the time. Hours of labor and focused thinking going into research and development that leads to clever but basically useless ideas. And this leads to a crucial question at the heart of many seemingly innovative yet ultimately unsuccessful ideas: Have I already decided what my customer wants without asking them?

It's crucially important to understand what people really value, and why they value it. I neither need nor want a $500 pair of shoes, or a $1,000 status bag, but millions of people consider them essential components of their lives. It would be incredibly foolish of me to discount their emotional and practical connections to these products just because they don't apply to my life. You have biases and you make judgments, just like all of us. Learning to step outside of them and not be sidetracked by your own opinions about the relative worth or value of a product is crucial. If you can't grasp this, you'll never be able to create an innovation that your customers either need or want.

EXPLORE, OBSERVE, ASK

I spend a lot of time in India, as most tech guys do. The subcontinent can be spectacularly disorienting for a Westerner. On a recent trip, I stayed in a blissfully air-conditioned, five-star hotel. Outside there was 100-degree heat, and the uniquely foul stench of Kolkata's open sewers and packed streets. Inside I had endless Western cable channels, purified water on tap, and a butler on call. Yet, the view out of my tenth-story window was more interesting than anything on the flat-screen TV. Just outside of the luxurious accommodations, hundreds of manual laborers worked in the sweltering heat to methodically dismantle a multistory building, brick by brick, all by hand. The workers moved with an almost hypnotic slowness, yet over the course of my three-day stay, the obsolete structure melted away before my eyes. This is one of the conundrums of understanding India, and indeed of understanding any relationship with people outside of your personal experience. The gulf between *your experience* of how things are done and *their experience* can be impossible to intuitively understand. You need to suspend your own assumptions about what an individual needs and wants, and get out there to explore, observe, ask questions, and allow your beliefs to be challenged and disproved.

On my return to the United States, I challenged my innovation team to think about emerging markets such as India. We talked a little about the huge gap between the Indian middle and upper class, as well as the lower-income workers who made up the bulk of the population. I described my driver in Kolkata. He was poor and had no education but was one of the most ambitious and focused men I've ever met. As a child, he had taught himself to speak English, an invaluable skill in India, by listening to the BBC on the radio. As a man, he was painstakingly schooling his children in the ABCs of spoken (though not written) English every evening. There was no reason for him to think he could claw his way out of poverty except for his own belief that it was possible. There are tens of millions of people like my driver in India— people who were born with nothing, but who are fiercely determined to boost their children out of the poverty they live in. And these men and women are doing it armed with nothing more than cell phones, an eye for opportunity, and creative, determined personalities. At the end of my trip, my driver asked for my e-mail and promised to stay in touch; I gave it to him gladly.

I asked the group to think about people like this. What do they want? What do they need? Their tiny annual incomes would typically put them out of range for our standard offerings. Should a company like mine want to engage with people who live so far outside of the Western experience of needs and wants? Well, yes. I think so. Look at it this way: The majority of the world's population has never owned a personal computer. From a purely marketing point of view, it's smart to focus on these people, because their situation is evolving and changing with the emergence of an ever-expanding middle class. They, or their children, will one day be technology customers, and I want them to be *our* customers.

I asked the group to think about one of the core Killer Questions we'll discuss in this chapter: *Who isn't using our product because of an assumption of skill or ability?* From the back of the conference room a voice asked, "How can we expect millions of people who can't read or write even in their own language, let alone English, to want a device that requires you to be literate to use it?" Bingo. With one quick question, the perspective of the entire team changed. How do you bring all the benefits of computing, the Internet, and communication potential to people who are literally unable to interact with the standard keyboard interface? How do you take away that barrier and help them leapfrog into a situation where they feel empowered to use a new device?

This was a classic slap-your-forehead-in-disbelief moment. The entire day, we'd been trying to shoehorn the product *we* wanted and needed—a typical PC setup—into the lives of people who had no use for it. Just like the rest of the industry, we had assumed that all you had to do to win this customer was build a PC cheaply enough. Eventually, we realized that thinking this way meant we were missing the point— that two overwhelming needs of the tens of millions of potential customers in the subcontinent are *relevancy* and *simplicity*. They don't want to update their Facebook page or send a tweet. What they want is a very simple machine that will allow them to communicate with their friends and families and educate their children.

We were approaching the problem with a limited point of view. We thought that our product lacked functionality, when in fact it had too much. The seeming complexity of navigating a standard PC scared users who had limited, or no, written-language skills. They didn't want to try early prototypes because they were afraid of the machines, and of humiliating themselves in front of our engineers. Their biggest fear was the keyboard, and the symbols on it. What should have facilitated them using the device was actually preventing it.

Once we finally started to talk to our potential customers, and look at the computer through their eyes rather than our own, we dramatically changed the features of the device. We asked the Killer Questions about what these potential customers actually needed and wanted, and the overwhelming answer was education, communication, and entertainment.

The product that was sparked by these questions—HP Dream-Screen 400—is a touch-screen device that fulfills these three needs with an easy-to-use, easy-to-understand touch interface. The keyboard and mouse are optional. It uses simple depictive symbols for those who don't understand Hindi or English to communicate with the user. Communication is a key issue in India, as well as many other emerging markets. The young emigrate to find opportunities abroad and, as a result, their families are split up. Their parents and grandparents typically don't have e-mail addresses, but most video-calling services like Skype require one to register for their product. This might seem like a small hurdle, but for people living in rural areas, it's insurmountable. How do we enable video calling with no assumption of literacy? Each Dream-Screen is issued a "phone number," rather than an e-mail address, and the user simply replicates the familiar experience of using a cell phone (press the green button to make a call) in order to make a video call.[1]

DreamScreen is in the process of being rolled out now. It has a number of other applications, such as allowing people to make simple transactions, like purchasing train tickets or paying their bills without waiting in line. Now, nobody *asked* for DreamScreen, and this is a key thing to think about as you use the Killer Questions to help generate ideas. Nobody came and said, *Hey, the illiterate customers in emerging markets could really use a simple application to facilitate communication, education, and entertainment in an easy and inexpensive manner.* None of the new customers who will soon be video-chatting with far-off relatives, or helping their children learn to read and write, thought that they needed or wanted this device. The automatic answer for the computer industry was to make a PC cheap enough so the emerging markets would buy it. But I believe that the vast majority of people who buy or are given a DreamScreen will quickly see it as an incredibly helpful tool in their lives. *They need it and they want it; they just don't know it yet.* And if you don't know you need or want something, then how can you ask for it?

This is a huge part of your task as an innovator. You need to be able to analyze and understand your potential customers' needs and wants before they are even able to clearly state them. Our Indian customers thought that standing in line for eight hours to pay a bill was simply the way things were done. It might have frustrated them, but they didn't think of it as a hassle that required a solution. It was up to us to see the possibilities here and deliver value. Time is the one universal commodity that we all prize. If I succeed in developing products to save people time, I build loyalty with a customer. If you are stuck in the innovation process, always remember that trying to save people time, thereby giving them a piece of their life back, is a great way to start. And never wait for your customers to ask you for a product, because if you wait for them to make a request, you are going to be stuck in a slow and incremental process of innovation.

So, how do you apply this lesson to your own experience?

This question—and the other questions in this section—are about understanding your customers and how their needs and wants change over time. Are they getting what they really need and want from you, or are you currently just an acceptable rather than ideal option to fill their needs? If it's the latter, then you're in trouble. Your clock is already ticking. As soon as a better option comes around, you will run the risk of losing your customers to them. Think of all the people who left Friendster and went to Facebook.

You must also be aware of and prepared for the possibility that *everything you assumed to be true yesterday may be disproved today.* This is the same whether you are overseeing a multibillion-dollar success or struggling to keep a family business alive. Ten years ago, the only way you could easily buy a plane ticket or book a hotel was to call a travel agent. Today? That entire industry, with a few specialized exceptions, is out of business. Why? Because the service that travel agents offer no longer fits the criteria of their *who*—customers looking to travel. Using a travel agent—at least for simple trips—now seems to add hassles rather than reduce them. Are you missing similar writing on the wall in terms of how you think about your customers?

Do you assume your customers will remain loyal to you because they have never told you their needs are changing?

If the answer is yes, then you are comfortable, and that's the most dangerous place to be. Why? Because the world—and especially the business world—is no longer a comfortable place. These are difficult and sometimes dangerous times, and complacency will kill you. Somewhere, right now, one of your competitors is having a DreamScreen moment. They are looking at the needs of your customers, and seeing a need that you've been too complacent to notice. In a very short period of time, you and your work are going to seem obsolete, unless you can beat them to the punch.

GETTING TO KNOW YOUR *WHO*   87

THE WHO *KILLER QUESTIONS*

There are hundreds of ways to break down your customers by demographic, but for the purposes of this book, I want to break them down in the simplest of ways. There are people who currently buy your products; people who could use your product but choose not to; and people who may buy your products in the future. It's easy to focus so intently on your current customers that you neglect the other groups, but that's a foolish choice. Have you ever gone out and actively sought a conversation with someone who used to like what you do, but now can't or won't buy your product? What about people who've never bought your product? I'm famous for seeking out opportunities to talk to people in Best Buy or other retail outlets who were looking at an HP product but chose another brand. If you want to understand why they put down your product and walked out with a competitor's, then you have to catch them in the moment. How else are you going to establish contact with these noncustomers?

Current Customers

Who is using my product in a way I never intended—and how?

Once a product has sold, it's pretty much out of your control. You may have an idea why people will buy it, and what they'll do with it, but the most you can ever do is guess. So why are you assuming that you know what your customer actually likes and values about your product, and how they use it?

One of my favorite blogs to read when I have downtime is Ikea hackers.net. Ikeahackers is just what it sounds like—a place where people can show off the ways in which they have repurposed and customized IKEA products. Some of the hacks are pretty impressive for a DIY home engineer (e.g., hanging a Mälm bed frame to the wall so it can flip up like a Murphy bed). Others are simpler (e.g., using printed curtains as fabric for a dress). Still others border on creative genius (e.g., the financially strapped parents of baby twins who created a feeding station by cutting two baby seat–sized holes in their IKEA kitchen table probably deserve a job in the design and innovation department).

These hackers are an extreme and sometimes funny example of "unanticipated uses," but I mention them here to reinforce an important point. It's easy to lock yourself into thinking that you fully understand who is using your product and how they are using it. There's a reason *Who is my customer?* is not a Killer Question: It sets you up to get an obvious and easy answer rather than forcing you to look outside of what you know to be true about the people who use and appreciate your products.

I myself have experienced this disconnect between how I *assume* my product is used and how it is actually used. My wife and I have a favorite bakery near where we live. The bakery is a small operation that makes great cakes and cupcakes. It's one of those places where there is always a line out the door on a Saturday afternoon, and my wife likes to take her time, which means that I spend a lot of time there too. About four years ago, we stopped in to grab a quick snack. As we contemplated vanilla versus chocolate, I noticed an HP TouchSmart set up on the corner of the counter; naturally, I went over to check it out. Now, the TouchSmart was the first PC that users could interact with by touch.[2] It's got a ton of applications. A busy, overscheduled family can use it as a hub computer for the home, running their calendars off of it and coordinating and communicating with one another. My wife uses hers while she cooks. She goes online to find recipes and coupons, or to check her e-mail. Sometimes she entertains friends with streaming music, or plays mahjong while they hang out in the kitchen. Designers and artists, such as the contestants on *Project Runway*, can use it to digitally sketch out images and ideas that need to be easily and instantly shared. However, in all our design and marketing meetings, it had *never* occurred to us that the TouchSmart could be used as a customer-facing kiosk in the retail market. Yet this is precisely what the owner of the bakery had done. He had bought a TouchSmart and written his own simple sales application. Each image—be it chocolate brownie or three-tier wedding cake—clicked through to an ordering screen. The customers could customize their order at their leisure, and place it without waiting in the interminable line.[3]

I was impressed, to say the least—and stunned that we had missed such an obvious use for something we'd worked so hard on. In the following weeks, I shared the story with anyone who would listen and suggested to them to go by the store and try it out for themselves. The teams took that input and developed a TouchSmart version that would support a kiosk offering. Today you'll see TouchSmart kiosks in action in a number of stores and public areas.

So, what should you take away from this story?

The person buying your product doesn't see it as an end solution. They see it as a *tool* that will help them solve a problem. For example, "*I have this tiny, tiny bakery. I can't hold or display everything I'm capable of offering. I'm losing out to bigger competitors. When I physically print out pictures and put them in a photo album for my customers, they get grimy and dirty and unappealing in a matter of weeks, yet I don't have the time to swap out pictures on a regular basis. I need something simple and efficient that will showcase my wares and take orders when I'm too busy.*"

Your customers look at what you're delivering as a tool—a tool for them to achieve their objective. Remember:

Your objective is to sell your product.
Their objective is to solve a problem.

I love being surprised on the job, and our local bakery showed me something I'd never considered. Now, its owner doesn't think he did anything that interesting. To him, it's a completely logical way to *address his need*. The fact that it never occurred to us to offer a TouchSmart as the solution didn't stop him from figuring it out for himself. So, figuring out who uses your product in a way you never intended can unlock new opportunities you would have never considered. You want to potentially double your sales? Go out there and investigate. Use the Sparking Points below to push yourself. You may be surprised.

SPARKING POINTS

- What problems and needs are you looking to address? Are you so tightly focused on what you believe your customers' problems and needs to be that you are missing out on potentially huge opportunities?
- How could you identify existing customers and observe how they use your product?
- Is there a way to give your potential customers an opportunity to play with and use your product without giving them specific parameters for how, when, and why they should use it? What do they come up with?

What are the criteria our customers use when selecting our product?

Do you know what your customers' reasons are for choosing your product over that of your competitor? When was the last time you really explored what does, or doesn't, motivate your customers?

Just a few years ago, a computer's screen size was one of the key decision factors for a person looking to buy a laptop. At the time, users required pretty minimal portability; the computer simply needed to be easy to move from nightstand to couch. Very few people were circumnavigating the globe with one in their carry-on. Laptops were essentially home or office devices, tethered to a power cord, and used primarily in one space. Users were focused on screen size as one of their key decision criteria. This was fueled by the television industry, which is still driven by the idea that bigger is better. And bigger equaled heavy, unwieldy, and battery-draining.

Of course, everything in business changes, and people's feelings about their laptops changed too. As laptops became more portable, they became more important on a personal as well as a professional level. They were no longer simply tools, but instead were morphing into extensions of who the person was as an individual. As laptops began to replace photo albums and CD collections, their owners began wanting them to reflect their tastes. At the same time, the Internet was exploding; Facebook, Twitter, and other social sites created an insatiable need to be online 24/7. The result was that personal technologies were expected to become more mobile.

Companies that saw this change coming won. HP realized that this fundamental social shift was happening and was able to anticipate it and continue to respond to it as it evolved. Customers were no longer buying computers based purely on their "speeds and feeds" (processor speed, size of hard disk, amount of memory, etc.). They actually wanted to go into a retail outlet and touch the machine—literally make a physical connection with it and see if it was "them." This was a sea change in how companies traditionally sold technology. One of our big competitors at the time made the bet that people wanted to buy their computers online. But this assumption missed a major social shift. The PC had become truly *personal,* and something that personal had to be bought *in person.* Think about when a friend asks to borrow your computer. If it's a desktop, fine, no problem. But your laptop? That's too personal. Your *whole life* is on it. And no matter how innocent your life is, you probably don't feel comfortable sharing it.

SPARKING POINTS

- When was the last time you asked a customer—not your marketing department, not your design department—what their criteria was for selecting a product? How do you ask them?
- Do your customers' buying habits align with what they claim their buying criteria are? For example, customers who claim to prioritize "green" but won't pay the premium?
- Are your criteria the same as your customers'? Are you designing your products to your criteria or your customers' criteria?

What are your unshakable beliefs about what your customers want?

One thing is to know what your customers *want* to do, another is to understand how they intend to get it done. It's easy to look at their goals and tell yourself that your product will match their needs. However, if you don't understand their internal philosophy about what they are doing and why they are doing it, you may find that they consider your product a complete failure. Competing companies can have the same goals but radically different strategies for achieving them. One of the clearest examples of this is the decades-long tussle between Airbus and Boeing. Both companies brought new long-range aircraft to market at more or less the same time. However, their respective offerings, the A380 and the 787 Dreamliner, reflect radically different ideas of how airlines will meet the needs and desires of their passengers.

Both companies understand the bottom line in their industry: getting CASM—cost per available seat mile—as low as possible. Both claim that their airplanes are highly fuel-efficient. Each also uses radically new technologies. The 787 is made of lightweight and high-durability composites and advanced aluminum alloy. The A380 boasts new integrated avionics systems in the cockpit, designed with fewer parts to push maintenance costs down, and its cockpit is designed to make it simpler for a pilot to switch between one Airbus model and another (giving airlines more flexibility with their crews). The onboard servers are robust enough to ensure that pilots can safely go "paperless." Crews can now ditch their bulky manuals and instead rely on the onboard computers to supply all the charts, logs, maintenance records, and performance calculations they need during a flight.[4]

However, the A380 and the 787 reflect completely different philosophies about how passengers will get from one destination to the other. The A380 is a hub-to-hub aircraft. Its size limits the airports it can service. You'll see it at places like London Heathrow, Los Angeles International, and Singapore's Changi Airport. You *won't* see it in Cleveland or Oslo or Fort Lauderdale. Airlines placing orders for the A380 are betting on two things. First, they assume that there will be a meaningful number of passengers who are simply looking to fly from hub to hub. Some examples might include the businessperson in London who needs to make a presentation in L.A. or the family in Sydney who wants to vacation in Paris. Second, they are betting that passengers will be willing to adhere to the old model of international transportation and connect from second- and third-tier airports via a hub.

Boeing is betting the other way. The 787 is small and nimble enough to service second-tier cities, yet its fuel efficiency allows it to function as a long-range aircraft. If Delta's or United's marketing department decides that Columbus, Ohio, needs nonstop service to Paris, they could do it with the Dreamliner. They couldn't do it with the A380.[5]

Airbus and Boeing both asked themselves the same Killer Question: *What are our unshakable beliefs about what our customers want?* Yet as soon as they'd asked that question and started to investigate it, they veered off in radically different directions based on what they believed their customers' needs and wants were.

The jury is out on who made the better bet, but my gut instinct is that both companies will struggle before eventually finding sufficient market share to justify their gamble. Innovation isn't always about beating your competitors. Each thinks they've satisfied one need, but really their customers have multiple needs. A goliath like United Continental will have needs for aircraft that can extract the most value from long-haul, large-volume routes while at the same time having aircraft that can service smaller airports. The bigger problem for manufacturers will be if airlines decide to embrace fleet homogeneity and restrict themselves to using *either* Airbus or Boeing.

SPARKING POINTS

- Do you have one "Who" or many? By this I mean, do your customers and your customers' customers (in this example, airline passengers) have the same criteria as one another, or do they have different needs and selection processes?

- How would you engage with your customers' customers? And how could you align their needs with what you are doing?
- How do you prioritize complementary and conflicting needs between your various customer groups? What is the selection process for getting an aggregated list of wants from across these groups?

Who is passionate about my product or something it relates to?

I've never shopped at the online craft marketplace Etsy.com. I'm not often in the market for hand-knitted iPod cozies, customized guitar cables, or the like. However, since 2005, Etsy.com has signed more than 400,000 merchants and nearly seven million users. Their annual sales figures for 2010 were $273 million.[6] Even more interesting to me is the level of passion that Etsy inspires. Etsy provides a way for talented people who produce quirky goods to go global. A young woman who customizes invitations out of vintage postcards would have struggled to find enough business before Etsy existed. By partnering with the website, she can benefit from its all-encompassing reach and make contact with enough serious customers to sustain and grow her business. On one level, Etsy provides a very simple service—allowing vendors to reach people who might not otherwise be aware of their products and make sales. On a deeper level, though, it allows entrepreneurs and customers who are passionate about something—often very niche—to find one another.

At the same time, Etsy provides the hope of freedom from the nine-to-five, and the opportunity for thousands of ambitious entrepreneurs to share their innovations with the world. Etsy doesn't promise its users success; it simply offers them a shot. The gamble and risk is all theirs. There is no physical exchange of goods between Etsy and its users, and the website makes its money by charging a commission on sales. The irony is that many users who break down the actual time they spend making a product versus what they can sell it for find they are lucky to make minimum wage. Other users find that their quirky one-offs are copied by factories or larger operations who can then undercut their prices on other, more commercial, retail sites. The relationship between Etsy and the store holder can be turbulent; users love the site, but some are growing increasingly frustrated that the core premise—you can only sell what you yourself make, crafting supplies, or vintage items—limits their potential profits. This ceiling means that the vast majority of users are doing this for one reason: passion. They love what they do, and they love/hate the website that allows them to do it.[7]

Passion makes the relationship between organization and customer volatile. Some companies can survive it (think of the outrage that briefly but noisily roils around every iteration of Facebook's operating agreement). Others misjudge the depths of their customers' feelings and can come perilously close to crumbling because of it. The Dutch bank ING recently enraged their customers by paying bonuses to bosses after it had been bailed out by the government. The banks' customers were so angered that they rallied on Twitter and threatened to withdraw their deposits en masse. Eventually, the bank reversed its position, the bonuses were rescinded, and order was restored.[8]

It will be interesting to see what Etsy evolves into, and whether it can keep the merchants who use it passionate in a positive way. It's possible Etsy will see them grow resentful, much like the original eBay sellers who railed against changes in the site's fee policy. For now, Etsy's services are enough to cement their merchants' passion and loyalty. Can you say the same about your business?

SPARKING POINTS

- Do you or your product inspire an emotional reaction from your users? Do they feel like they couldn't get by without what you do? Why or why not?
- Can you tell the difference between a customer who feels frustrated that he has to use your product, and one who is grateful that your product is there and available to him?
- What are you doing to understand this emotional connection?

Who complains about my product?

A few years ago, a passenger complaint letter to Virgin Atlantic circulated around the web. It was very long, fully illustrated with photos, clearly somewhat tongue-in-cheek, and very funny, but it made a few good points about the bad food and surly service this particular passenger had experienced. Almost three years later it still occasionally shows up as one of the most-read stories at telegraph.co.uk.[9] In 2009, another disgruntled passenger created a music video about how United baggage handlers had broken his $3,500 guitar. He uploaded the song to YouTube, and to date it has been viewed more than ten million times. United's customer service department, which had originally denied him any kind of compensation, quickly changed their minds as the video went viral. They adjusted their tone from defensive to humorous and held a meeting with the passenger. Eventually, the airline made a charitable donation to a jazz school in his name.[10] The problem is that none of their existing, former, or potential customers care that United eventually resolved the customer complaint. All they remember is that it took a funny song and nine million YouTube hits to get the airline to do the right thing. United responded about as nimbly and elegantly as a dad trying to name-check Jay-Z at his kid's birthday party. Not pretty.

The point is, it's easier than ever to find out what your customers are thinking and saying about you these days. It's also much easier for their opinions to go viral, so it's imperative that you respond to them with the same speed and immediacy they use to critique you.

Social networking sites have fundamentally changed the nature of the customer complaint. Customer complaints are morphing from one-off exchanges between a customer and a service representative into ongoing conversations, often in real-time, visible to the public, and open to anyone who cares to comment. By monitoring these sites (I currently focus on Facebook and Twitter, but I might be tracking others by the time you read this), you can hear what your customers are saying about you, without them even being aware that their opinions are being heard.

I recently found out about a notebook hinge problem through Twitter. How? I have the TweetDeck app up all the time, and I use it to search for any tweet related to various topics I'm interested in. One day I was sitting in my office and a customer tweeted that he was having a problem with his HP notebook. The complaint got my attention. I put down what I was doing and went to respond to the tweet, but before I could even get my hands on the keyboard another customer replied, "It's a known problem, and they have has a repair protocol." A few seconds later he used a second tweet to direct the customer to the customer-service number.

What? There I was, the CTO of the PC division, and even I had no idea that we (a) had a problem or (b) had a solution. Yet here was a customer who was at least two steps ahead of me.

I grabbed the phone, dialed the product team, and asked, "What's this I'm hearing about a problem with one of our notebooks?" The person on the other end nearly had a heart attack. His department was carefully preparing the internal e-mail describing the problem, and suddenly the CTO of the division is breathing down his neck, asking him what the heck is going on.

The reality is, you can no longer keep problems like this off the radar, either within your organization or with your customers. Your only option is to engage with the people who care enough to make their feelings public. And don't stop at simply resolving an issue. The customers who take time out to post their opinions, or direct others to solutions, are the ones who have actually thought about what you do, and how you do it. Odds are, if they've complained about what you're doing, they've also thought about ways to do it better. So ask them.

SPARKING POINTS

- How do you receive and respond to customer complaints? Do you ever see them directly, or are they filtered through a specific department?

- Are your customers having a real-time conversation on Twitter, Facebook, or Yelp about what you are doing, and what you are doing to engage? Do you have the flexibility to respond immediately to these conversations?
- Can you identify—off the top of your head, right now—the most common complaints your company receives?
- How do these complaints make their way into future products?

Potential Customers

Who does not use my product because of my assumptions about their skill or ability?

Earlier in the chapter, I mentioned DreamScreen. By the time *Beyond the Obvious* is published, DreamScreen will have been rolled out across India. Have a look at that section again. Computers—and the way people use them—are my core business. Understanding this connection is what I do, yet even I missed the central disconnect between what I do and what my customers needed and wanted. I did not understand their criteria for choosing my product, or the hassles that would need to be eliminated in order for it to be worthwhile. It took a different set of eyes, and a different perspective, to help me make the cognitive leap.

SPARKING POINTS

- What skills or abilities are required by your customer in order to use your product?
- Who isn't buying your product because they don't possess the skills to use it?
- What would happen if you had to sell to them? How would you modify your product to meet their skills and abilities?
- Have you ever given people who you think aren't your potential customers a chance to play and interact with your product? What kind of feedback do you get when you do this?

Who does not understand how to use my product because it has too few or too many features and functions?

A few years ago, a friend's teenage daughter decided she wanted to learn to sew. Her parents, thrilled at her interest in such a wholesome hobby, promised to buy her any sewing machine that caught her eye. Her mom had been an avid seamstress in her youth and clearly remembered the machine she had learned on, a heavy iron Singer that did two things: sewed a straight stitch forward and in reverse.

Later that day, their daughter came home with her new machine. She told her parents about all its functions. It could sew zigzags and patterned stitches with two needles at the same time. It could make buttonholes and embroider. It could do everything short of design the dress for you. For the next two days, the daughter locked herself in her bedroom and sewed. Or tried to. The machine's endless options confused her. Eventually, she cracked and asked for help, but even her mom's skills were no match for the hundreds of stitch variations. She promised her daughter she'd teach her to sew, but the machine had to go. Instead, they went up to the attic, got out the old Singer, and contented themselves with forward and reverse.

Sometimes innovation is less about adding functionality than it is about providing the essentials of what an individual actually needs. A meaningful breakthrough can come when you recognize that your customer might be comfortable with less, rather than more. Often you can actually charge *more* for *less* if the simplicity and ease-of-use is worth more than complex and unnecessary features. In the early '90s, the Palm Pilot and the Apple Newton were released at roughly the same time. The Apple Newton promised users the world, including handwriting recognition. It was loaded with functionality, but way ahead of the technology available at the time. The end result was that none of its many features actually worked very well.[11] Conversely, the Palm did only a few things, but it did them superbly. It had fewer features, and less capability, but it proved to have a much higher value on the marketplace. Its less was actually more. The Newton slunk off into tech history, and Apple learned a useful lesson about making sure that the functions they offered were usable by the customer.

SPARKING POINTS

- What are the 20 percent of your product features that are used 80 percent of the time? Are the other 80 percent needed or could you remove them?
- Are you missing features from your product that are part of the critical buying criteria for your customers?
- How are you engaging with your customers to quantify the value they associate with each feature?

What are the unanticipated uses of my product?

Not all interesting discoveries have an obvious application. If you believe you have something, but you're not sure what exactly it's going to be good for, don't give up. Many innovations languished in labs for years until they were matched to a product. Teflon was invented in 1938, but it didn't coat its first pan till 1954.[12] The Post-it note was built on the back of some not-very-good glue. Its inventor believed it might have value, but it took him five years to get any support for the concept, or find a potentially profitable use for it.[13] HP had a breakthrough with a super-accurate thermometer that was created in the HP Labs. Despite its accuracy, there was no clear use for the device until it was used to measure fluctuations in ocean temperature. The resulting data is a key component in ongoing discoveries about the rising temperatures in the oceans.[14]

If an idea is new, interesting, and has unique properties, you will find a use for it, along with customers who will want to buy the end product. Have patience; it can take a while before the customer need emerges.

SPARKING POINTS

- Do you have customers who can benefit from the unanticipated uses of a product? How could you identify a potential group of such customers?
- What's the most unusual way you've ever seen your product utilized?
- How could you encourage other users to find out about the unanticipated uses of your products or services?

Who do I not want to use my product now, but may want to in the future?

We tend to assume that any customer is a good customer. However, if you find that you're working like crazy and have a solid and reliable customer base, but you're *still* not making the profits you expected, then ask the Killer Question, *Who do I not want to use my product?*

Do you remember back when dial-up Internet service first started to transition to the mainstream? In the early '90s, companies like AOL, CompuServe, and EarthLink began offering access to the web that was billed by the minute. The more you used, the more you paid. Logical, right? These three companies essentially offered the same product on the same terms. Very quickly, the people who used the services they offered divided into two camps. The majority logged on once or twice a day, checked their e-mail, read some sports stats or gossip, and logged off. However, a small minority logged on for hours or days at a time. These people quickly ran up bills in the thousands. Now—pop quiz—is this a good thing or a bad thing for your business? These high-volume users *love* your service, but paradoxically their passion for what you offer will almost inevitably force them to stop, or drive them into an untenable situation if they try to continue. So, if you were running AOL, CompuServe, or EarthLink, what would you do? Continue the same pricing structure that strongly disfavored your most ardent users, or figure out some way to continue improving profits without punishing the people who really, really love what you do? In other words, would you decide to keep or push out these high-use customers?

In the end, AOL was the first to take a radical step to address these questions. In 1996, they switched from a pay-per-minute system to a flat-rate fee.[15] This was a daring and audacious move because they risked seriously alienating low-usage customers who were used to paying less than twenty dollars a month. On the flipside, they had to massively upgrade their infrastructure in order to accommodate demand. AOL was bombarded with complaints about busy signals and slow speed. Users joked that AOL stood for "Always Off Line." For a short while it looked like they might have made a poor decision. However, this new flat fee addressed a fundamental fear that even low-usage customers had with the old pricing formula. Namely, not knowing how much the monthly cost was going to be. AOL's new strategy took away the stress that came with worrying about the bill. Parents no longer had to hover over their kids and nag them about getting offline. The result was that the company shot ahead of all of the others and became the leading ISP through the early 2000s. The other companies—EarthLink, CompuServe, and Prodigy—quickly copied AOL's new pricing structure, but AOL had the huge advantage of being the first mover. Their competitors looked like copiers, whereas AOL looked like a game-changer. They won that round.

In the early days of the mobile phone industry, telecom companies grappled with similar issues, with their cell-phone customers hogging the bandwidth in a given area. Parents would toss a cell phone into their baby's crib, dial another cell phone from it, and keep the line open all night, using it as a baby monitor under the "free evenings and weekends" pricing promotions. More recently, people have used their smartphones as jury-rigged security systems by streaming constant live footage from their office or home security cameras while they are on vacation. Anyone who's experienced problems with AT&T's network in urban areas can understand why this might be an issue. So, are these customers abusive? Do you want them? Should you penalize them for using vastly more than their share of the network and compromising connectivity for other users?

If I were still working in the wireless industry, I'd be looking at ways to understand and migrate the high-volume users into an elite program. My feeling is that if someone loves what you do, and uses it habitually, then that's a customer you want to hold on to. If what you see as abuse is actually foresight—being ahead of a curve—then you might be looking at a future revenue stream rather than a problem. You just haven't figured out how to separate out this use, give it its own program apart from the existing customer agreement, and monetize it. In this situation, it's worth taking the time to figure out a way to find a satisfactory medium between their needs and yours.

SPARKING POINTS

- Do you have customers who consistently take "more than their share" of what you are offering? Is this a problem for you?
- If it's a problem, why? Is it compromising your other customers' experience, or taking an inordinate amount of time for you to deal with?
- Are these people really abusing you and what you do—or have they simply found a new way to use your product? Are they finding a value you hadn't anticipated in what you do? Are they showing you an unanticipated use that you could monetize?

Who am I not selling to because I think they can't or won't pay for my product?

Price is king, right? "Build 'em cheap and stack 'em high" is practically the motto of most segments of the tech industry (naturally, there are some notable exceptions). It's certainly a core assumption about what the majority of customers want.

For example, $320 is a huge sum of money for a middle- or lower-income Indian family, but it hasn't stopped sales of DreamScreen. Our customers see the value that DreamScreen brings to their lives. The price, though steep, makes sense. Never kill an idea because you assume your customers can't afford it. If the value the product brings to their life justifies the cost, they will find a way to make the purchase.

Your first concern should be to make it relevant; your second, to make it affordable.

Remember that in many cases the customer is not evaluating the perceived worth of your product solely on price, but more on value. They ask themselves, *"What do I get for the money that I spend?"* If you're getting tripped up in trying to understand if your customer will perceive your product as "expensive," ask yourself if you are mistakenly thinking of price and value as being the same thing. Price and value are *not* the same thing; if there is sufficient value in the product, the customer will find a way to save for or finance their purchase.

People will find a way to pay for the things that are important to them, and *important* is a purely subjective thing. Look at the organic food market. Vegetables that are certified as organic cost an average of 50 percent more than nonorganic. Organic milk and meat are almost twice the price of commercially raised products. Now, everybody benefits from healthy food, but there is still no definitive study showing that an organic head of broccoli is dramatically healthier than its commercially raised counterpart. Yet millions of people regard the extra cost of organic food as part of the *cost of doing business*, or raising their family. Organic matters to them, and they'll prioritize it, even if it means cutting out other items from their budget.

There are other ways to give a customer access to products that are theoretically too expensive for them to purchase. In the last five years, businesses that allow women to rent luxury items for monthly fees have become a huge trend. Bagborrowandsteal.com allows a user to rent a Chloé handbag for $225 a month. At the end of the month, the customer returns the bag and receives a new designer item in its place. The bag would cost her more than $1,500 to buy new. Other companies rent designer dresses for roughly ten percent of the purchase price. The woman rents it, wears it, and returns it a few days later.

There are questions here about whether these smaller rental companies are harming large luxury brands by devaluing the products they rent, or benefiting them by extending the brands' reach to a new audience. There are good reasons why Gucci, for instance, does not rent their dresses and bags directly to a customer. The person who purchases a dress for several thousand dollars does not want to see it worn by her assistant for a tenth of the price. However, if that assistant then goes out and *buys* the perfume to go with the *rented* dress, and begins a longer-term relationship with a brand like Chloé or Gucci or Louis Vuitton, then maybe it ultimately benefits these brands. Either way, it's an interesting and innovative way to tap into people's desires, and provide them with the things they need and want.

SPARKING POINTS

- Is the expense of your product in some way central to how your customers think or feel about it?
- Would you benefit from having more people able to afford what you sell, or does its exclusivity magnify your potential customers' desire to buy it?

Future Customers

Do you remember when your family had one telephone in the house? It was probably wired through to the kitchen, and maybe the parents' bedroom. If the kids were lucky, they might get an extension when they were deemed responsible enough to deserve it. A phone number was a fixed thing; it belonged to a location, not a person. It rang in your house, not in your pocket. You paid rent on each phone in the house. Surprisingly, there are still people who are paying rent to their telephone company for phones. Think of that key transition—that moment when houses stopped having telephone numbers and people started having them instead. Sure, the older generation still likes the security of a home line, but how many people under the age of thirty do you know who care? This is a huge shift that happened very quickly, and for the most part caught the communications industry off guard. The telephone companies weren't looking beyond their current customers' needs. As a result, they missed that there were new customers coming who didn't need what they were offering.

The communication industry's key problem now is how to either create or maintain some sense of customer loyalty. Do you care who provides your Internet or phone line at home? No? Neither do I. They're all the same, right? By bundling services, the telecom giants are creating loyalty based on price. However, I'd argue that this is not a particularly strong bond. Right now, I get a decent deal from AT&T on my Internet, TV, data, and phone. But if the only connection I feel to them is that they are cheapest, then I'm going to switch the second another carrier can do better.

In order to stay on top of your "future customer needs," you must identify, watch, and understand your future customers.

What customer segment will emerge in five years that doesn't exist today?

HP has an Executive Briefing Center where corporate clients come to be briefed about the latest technologies and products that are either in development or about to hit the market. Now, technically, this service is for *them*. HP offers them information and opportunities to stay ahead of the newest advancements in technology. But, as is my way, I saw an opportunity for me, too. I would get in there and ask these executives questions. I was always curious about their priorities—the things that were the most important to them right then. Not just in terms of HP products, but more generally. What was going on in the organizational structure of their business? What was new? What was changing? For good or bad?

When we would break for lunch, I would use this time to get my finger on the pulse of what mattered to them, both as individual businesspeople and as representatives of their company. If I was lucky, I would hit on something important—perhaps a shift in the unique characteristics of their customers.

In late 2008, I started to notice something very interesting. Executive after executive—from wildly different businesses—mentioned that they were experimenting with ways to provide new employees with computers to use in the workplace. Some were going to the extreme of assuming that it's not the company's responsibility to provide the tools its employees need to do the job. These businesses are making the radical shift to deciding that a laptop is more like a car or a cell phone. It's something that an employee needs to be part of the modern workforce—something, in other words, that the employee must offer as part of the value package they bring to an employer.

I wondered if I had stumbled onto an early trend. I asked the next five clients I worked with at the Executive Briefing Center, and they all acknowledged that they, too, were looking for ways to change personal computer ownership. For me, five customers with the same idea was validation, and as soon as I got back to the office, I hashed out the idea on paper. Clearly, there was about to be a huge and unexpected shift in how corporations would be buying IT, and yet it had never popped up on anyone's radar screen. By acting quickly, we'd have enough of a lead to be ready to respond in a few years, when this change had gone through in a widespread fashion.

Now, the interesting thing is that in situations like this, you can often get a ton of pushback from the very people who should have jumped at the chance to move on your insight. With any radical idea, you will see the corporate antibodies come out of the woodwork, giving all the standard reasons why the idea will "never happen." Remember, the fundamental assumption of the corporate antibody is that the future will be the same as today.

Your customers are going to change. It's that simple. Don't ever turn down a chance to be on top of that change, just because you don't want to deal with it. And if you get pushback, push harder. Have faith in what you are learning by asking the Killer Questions. Don't let others' hesitation keep you from pursuing the changes you and your company will need to make to be ready for the unavoidable changes in your customers.

SPARKING POINTS

- How are you anticipating shifts in your customer segments?
- How have your customer segments changed over the last five years?
- What are the people who will be your customers in five years excited about today?

How will you identify and reach customers in five years?

Every hot trend reaches a point I like to call the "Uncle Larry moment." You know what I mean. It's the juncture where one of your older relatives announces he's taken up something that had seemed cutting edge, futuristic, and exciting up till that second. Facebook and Twitter have long passed the Uncle Larry moment. MySpace passed it years ago. If you've successfully embraced social media, fantastic. If you've embraced it, but failed to make it work for you, then let's talk.

It's critical to constantly reconsider and, if necessary, change the way you are communicating with your customers. Look at how you are finding them, and how they are finding you. Are you applying an old-world mentality to a new-world technology?

Don't rely on today's version of social media; ask yourself what form tomorrow's Twitter will take. Will you be able to recognize and embrace it in a timely fashion?

It's critical to be on board with these social evolutions as they happen and not be the last person to the party. Again, the only way to really gauge which company will be the next Groupon, and which will quickly disappear, is to find out what the people around you are actually using. I knew Groupon was going to be a success when I heard my wife mention it to three different friends within twenty-four hours. She became a vocal fan and recruiter of others to try the service. I'm not a shopper, and I don't have the interest to comparison shop for anything other than big-ticket purchases. But she does, and Groupon works for her.

How are you going to communicate with your customers as the nature of the methods you use to interact with them changes?

A decade ago, a lot of companies started reaching out to their customers through blogs. Now it's apps. Everyone thinks that if they offer their customer an app for their phone, it will somehow create loyalty, generate business, and basically do the heavy lifting of communicating with their clientele for them. This is the worst kind of backward thinking. Sure, there are some great apps out there, but who wants a hundred different corporate apps on their smartphone? If you're going to use social media to engage with your customer (and by now it really shouldn't be a question of *if*), then you have to be an early adopter. If that's just not going to happen within your corporate structure, then at least don't be a follower. Don't watch to see what's working for other people and then copy them a year later. Don't be the last corporation to get a Twitter account or ask people to like them on Facebook. You have to take risks and decide if the next thing for you is going to be "social commerce," "augmented intelligence," or "sensor networks."

SPARKING POINTS

- Where are your customers going to spend their time in the next five years?
- What new emerging media is going to be competing for that time in five years (e.g., immersive media)?
- How will you communicate with your customers in these new types of social spaces?

What will future customers' buying criteria be?

A big part of my business is being aware of, and responding to, the life cycles of my industry and my customers. Some of these are easy to see; you only need a cursory understanding of the effect of OPEC on gas prices in the early '70s to understand why cars became more fuel efficient in that decade. Other reasons are harder to see. Some criteria can be "faddish," based on things such as color or brand. Others are based on external influences. For years the cell-phone industry fought to offer the smallest, thinnest possible phone. That's what customers wanted. Now those same customers are prioritizing access to the web over the size of the phone. This has reversed what was seen as a key and unshakable evolution trend toward smaller phones. Now customers want larger phones with bigger screens. Sometimes trends can be reversed by something completely outside your control. Something that changes the buying decision. What will these same consumers want as they get older? Will full web access and streaming music and video be a priority, or will their needs change as their eyesight and hearing fade?

Remember the *cycle* part of "life cycle." You may lose the connection with your customers at certain stages of their lives but regain it later. It's like the young man who buys a sports car when he gets out of college, trades it in for a minivan when he marries and has kids, and finally reverts back to a sports car as an empty nester. Don't assume that a customer is lost forever just because they've shifted their allegiances for the time being. If you can maintain some kind of link during the years they are not using your product, you still have a good shot at winning them back again when their needs and your services match up better.

We are rarely fortunate enough to know exactly how our customers' needs will change; we simply know they will. The easiest way to anticipate how radically your customers' needs and wants may evolve is to look at the past. Think about how our expectations of personal transportation have evolved. When your great-grandfather needed transportation, he might have looked for a sturdy horse and a well-made saddle. Your father wanted a car. My first vehicle was a motorcycle, as it was all I could afford at the time.

Simply understanding which products fell into and out of use isn't enough. You need to consider the entwined relationship between people and the products that allow their lives, and their expectations about their lives, to evolve. The more our grandparents and parents came to rely on going wherever they wanted, whenever they wanted, the more their lives were built around this very premise. Your great-

great-grandfather couldn't have sustained a traditional family life if he lived fifty miles from his place of work, yet now we assume that this is a standard setup for a commuter. Understanding this constant back-and-forth between the products we use and how they affect our lives can help you predict how this relationship will evolve in the future. What will personal transportation look like ten years in the future? Will new traffic-flow and work-scheduling solutions allow greater mobility and the continuation of a suburban lifestyle? Or will people become so frustrated with ever-worsening commutes that they return to dense urban areas or flee to rural ones? Could these changes affect your customers' buying decisions, and if so, what are you going to do about it?

What other cycles like this can you start to anticipate now? How are your customers building new ways of living their lives based on new products and assumptions? Stay close to your existing customers and talk to them. Realize that they might not understand their own needs; it's up to you to ask the Killer Questions and get a more nuanced perspective on what is driving them and their lives. Their buying decisions are not going to be the same three or four years from now. So long as you keep asking "Who are they, what do they want, and why do they want it?" you stand a good chance of staying ahead of the inevitable changes.

SPARKING POINTS

- What are the ways your future customers' lives are changing?
- How will that influence what they buy?
- What will they abandon and no longer purchase as their lives change?

As long as you keep investigating your customer and never assume you know what their needs and wants are, you will be in a position to anticipate the inevitable changes in their buying decisions. Make it a habit to seek out your customers, but also to seek out the people who *aren't* buying what you sell. Talk to your kids and their friends; actively try to understand how they are different from you. Keep engaging, keep getting out there, keep asking the Killer Questions, and you'll have the perspective and clarity to understand who these people are, what they want, and how you can build a longstanding relationship with them.

CHAPTER 7

What Is Your What?

This chapter is, quite simply, about what you create—be it a physical product, the product as experience, or product as a service—and how you are going to keep developing and evolving it over the course of its life cycle. It's easy to have your blinders on regarding what the core value of your product is, but you need to be alert. That core value is constantly shifting. A customer who loves your car for its roomy interior today may love it for its low gas mileage tomorrow. If you don't understand where the core value is in your product, and what it is about your product that is (or isn't) connecting with customers, then you are not prepared for the ever-shifting marketplace of the future.

Odds are you think you know *what* you are selling, but do you know *why* your customers value your product? What makes it an essential purchase for your customer? So, what exactly is your *What*? The answer probably seems obvious, but take a second and really think about it: Is what you're offering something unique and necessary to your customer? Also, how are you going to focus in on the core nugget of what you do and what you're really good at, and expand on it in the future?

THE WHAT *KILLER QUESTIONS*

How do you decide on the factors that go into evolving your current products, or developing new ones for the future? These Killer Questions are about looking at the products you have in the hopper now, or will have in the next few years, and ensuring that they offer the maximum possible value to the customer, thereby delivering the maximum possible return to your organization.

Current Products

Could I create a standardized offering of a custom product?

One of the first products I created as a software developer was a touch-typing program called Typing Instructor.[1] This was back in 1985, and at that time there was no such thing as a standard PC. Instead you owned a specific brand and had access to the programs that had been written specifically for that make, whether IBM, Wang, or DEC. Each of these companies was attempting to create lock-in for their third-party software developers. If a user wanted a specific application, they needed to own the computer for which it was written.

Now, was this a good thing or a bad thing? All of these brands approached the problem in unique ways. Compaq, a dinky start-up in the 1980s, had the most expansive philosophy about building their business. The team at Compaq realized that to win against the industry strategy of creating unique, proprietary PCs, they must push for PC uniformity. They decided to make their products compatible with IBM. Similarly, IBM licensed MS-DOS, a Microsoft operating system designed specifically for their PCs, a decision that subsequently made a fortune for Bill Gates.[2]

On the other hand, companies like DEC and Wang thought they could create some unique differentiators that would make the software developers come to their platforms first. Wang was especially notorious for wanting to keep their programs proprietary.[3] Because the PC manufacturers were in a fight to dominate the market and win over the largest market share as quickly as possible, locking a customer into using their brand and making it as hard as possible for the customer to switch in the future seemed like a good idea.

One of my first jobs in computer engineering was with a company called Individual Software. I was twenty-four at the time and married with a kid when Individual called me. I knew these guys, and I had faith that they were going to do interesting work, and that it would be a good place to get in on the ground floor of a booming industry. I talked to my wife and we packed up our lives and drove west to Silicon Valley. Individual had some ideas for programs, and one of the first that seemed to have real potential was a simple program to teach touch-typing. Think about it—home PC use was exploding. Even if a user didn't need touch-typing at work, they were soon going to start wanting it at home. My colleagues at Individual and I got together and started throwing ideas around. Once we'd decided what kind of program we wanted to write, the second question was *What PC are we going to write it for?*

This was in the early days of Silicon Valley. Individual was at the crucial phase of a young, start-up company. We had the resources to make one or two moves, and if these moves didn't work, we were going to be out of cash and out of luck. One of the biggest stumbling blocks was the fact that in the mid-'80s there were easily a dozen different major PC manufacturers in widespread use. While each of these companies used the same OS, they all tweaked it by adding custom code to MS-DOS to make it work with their hardware. Clearly, some of these PC companies were going to fail, but there was no guarantee about which company was going to win. Since each of these PCs required its own version of your program, how could you decide which one to write for? Individual needed to get products out to as many users as possible to survive, but any choice we made was automatically going to eliminate the majority of our potential customers. Writing a separate program for each operating system was not financially possible. We had limited research and development (R&D) dollars to spend, and the future of our company was riding on making the best choice. So what do you do?

Traditionally, a company like ours would write a program, and then spend a lot of R&D dollars on porting (or rewriting) it to work with as many operating systems as possible. However, this wasn't going to work for us. We couldn't afford to do it. We had the budget to write the program once, but if we only wrote it once we weren't going to be able to sell enough copies to ever make a profit. How could we take those R&D dollars and put them into an approach that would allow us to create a standard product once, rather than multiple custom versions?

We turned this question over and over in our heads. Finally, we did what innovators throughout history have done in this kind of situation. We said, "Forget the obvious solution," and we decided to take a crazy gamble. Instead of writing a program specifically for an IBM or a Wang, we took the same amount of money and created a software engine that essentially worked as a universal translator, and allowed the same program to run on any of the existing PCs.

While the industry, thankfully, has moved away from proprietary PC platforms, developing the translation engine rather than worrying about the program was a 180-degree turn from what was the norm at the time. It could have killed our company and left us all out on the street, yet it paid off. If you go into a big-box computer store today, you can still buy a copy of Typing Instructor more than twenty-five years after it was first written. It's not hip, it's not glamorous, but it works—really well. And that's what counts.

SPARKING POINTS

- What custom products could be transformed into a standard, mass-market offering?
- Could you keep the feel of and desire for custom products while expanding the number of customers who can afford it?
- How could you disrupt the structure and finance of an industry based on custom products?

How can I take advantage of emerging trends and fads?

"Weak signals" are the equivalent of a canary in a coal mine. They are the unspoken needs and wants of your customers, and they are also the arrows pointing to what your customers are going to need and want in the future, even if they themselves don't know it yet. If you pay attention to the weak signals, they'll give you the heads-up that something radical, and possibly uncomfortable, is coming your way.

You're not going to find them on the front page of a newspaper or in an industry analyst report. If you are pitching me an idea that's already been covered in an analyst report, forget it. You're too late. If you're pitching me a weak signal that you uncovered during a customer conversation or found in an obscure magazine or local paper you picked up on a layover on the other side of the world, OK, I'm interested. I find weak signals in the comments on a blog post, or in a casual observation that my kid's friends might make at dinner one night. A weak signal is something that seeps into the zeitgeist almost unnoticed. One week you've never heard of it, the next it's a fitness or shopping craze that all your friends have signed up for. And when weak signals intersect with the "Rule of Five," I really start to take notice. Essentially, the Rule of Five means that I've heard the same core message that "something new is happening here" five times within a short time span.

Here's a good example of how a weak signal about a cultural shift brought me to the moment when I said to myself, "I need to think about this." I've always been interested in graffiti, and I make a point to observe it when I'm traveling. It's an interesting look into the thoughts and interests of groups of people I will never interact with. It's an elaborate, and sometimes quite visually stunning, way of saying "I was here, this is who I was, and this is what I was thinking at the time." I remember visiting a small and obscure French castle, well off the tourist route. On the walls of the dungeon, someone had chiseled the outline of his hand and carved words to the effect of PIERRE WAS HERE. It dated to the late fourteenth century. People have always felt a deep-seated need to announce their presence—no matter how fleeting—in the world.

Fast-forward to the early 1990s. I buy lots of completely random magazines when I'm traveling—anything from Eastern European news magazines to music papers to local 'zines and newspapers. Years ago, I picked up a copy of a magazine called *Graphotism* in the old Tower Records store in Piccadilly Circus. It's a magazine aimed at graffiti artists. The magazine showed pictures of graffiti art from all over the world but also highlighted gallery exhibitions built around graffiti. What was once considered a crime was now being shown in galleries, being sold to early adopters and eventually ending up on the walls of people's condos. Now, this was all interesting, and it appealed to me as a former architecture and design student, but it didn't necessarily herald that a big change was happening. The magazine and the gallery exhibits were weak signals, but they were still isolated weak signals.

Jumping to the early 2000s, I became aware of a new weak signal, a mobile application called Tag and Scan. Tag and Scan allows you to leave digital graffiti. The app lets you type out opinion messages, such as an opinion of a local restaurant, and digitally suspends them in front of destinations. This is graffiti set to maximum. It used to be that if a restaurant was tagged with unflattering graffiti, the owner could scrub it off. But with digital graffiti, you can now leave a virtual message, and the owner can't do anything about it. This transition from obscurity or niche to the edge of mainstream is the first hint of broad adoption of something new. Transitions like this are hard to see but when you do find them, jump on them. The Tag and Scan application was an early and limited experiment, but I recognized that this program hinted at something bigger.

Today, we have seen an explosion of location-based services like Foursquare, Yelp, and more recently Facebook. They are the direct successor to Tag and Scan, and they tap into the same desire to be known, to be remembered, and to have your opinion felt and heard—the same desire that causes people to chisel their name in rock, or tag a wall with an aerosol can. Nothing is worse than being anonymous and unnoticed, and each of these examples evolved from the thing that came before. The leap from physical to digital graffiti was a catalyst to all kinds of location-based services.

Of course, the trouble with weak signals is that they are exactly that—weak. Until the Rule of Five kicks in, it's easy to ignore them, or tell yourself that nothing's going to happen with these trends. Which is why I'm not telling you about my big launch of my hugely successful product that is a direct descendant of Tag and Scan. Despite my fascination with graffiti culture, I missed the ways in which the "I was here" sentiment could be adapted to social technology. Now, this oversight was more to do with the slow pace of adoption rather than underestimating the importance of the graffiti mind-set. Keep in mind that we are talking about a weak signal that took almost fifteen years to go from fringe to broad adoption. It's easy to get distracted and fall into the trap of thinking that it will never make it.

So, what's the next trend or fad that is giving off a weak signal?

SPARKING POINTS

- What hints did you get before major changes in customer behavior, product innovations, or shifts in the marketplace occurred?
- What nonstandard input (e.g., reading fringe magazines) do you use as a way to find weak signals?
- How do you share these emerging trends within your organization?

How can I eliminate customer hassles and create unique benefits for customers?

Why do people choose you over your competitors? Or, vice versa? How do you go about eliminating a hassle or creating a benefit to your customer if there is no obvious reason for them to pick you over your competitor?

I pretty much hate flying these days, which is unfortunate, because I log a minimum of a quarter-million miles every year. Travel is at best a neutral experience, and at worst an awful one, but that's probably not news to you. Of course, the interesting idea here is how customers have adapted to the ever-degrading experience of travel. In fact, every new hassle of flying is absorbed into the "new normal" and accepted by travelers relatively quickly. Who would have thought that the flying public would accept more intense and invasive warrantless pat-downs than some police forces are authorized to do—especially when there is no evidence that these searches actually accomplish anything? But the public has.

The point is that customers are generally quick to accept a reduction in "pleasantness" and an increase in hassles, especially when the individual businesses that comprise an industry present a united front on the issue (for example, seemingly coordinated price hikes or near simultaneous service downgrades). As frustrating as these situations are, they also present an opportunity. Low expectations and hassles are something to take advantage of, because they are an opportunity to surprise and excite your customer. If you can twist these hassles and make people pleased to get an experience that feels new and exciting, or even just approximates old standards of service, they'll be happy. Often, just acknowledging the reality of the downgraded experience instead of trying to pass it off as something done "for your convenience" helps mitigate customer frustration and reduces the perception of a hassle. One of my favorite airlines right now is Southwest, which is funny because I'm guaranteed an economy seat on them, rather than the business or first-class seat I get on a legacy carrier. Why do I like Southwest? They're pretty much perkless, but the minimal service they offer is given in a straightforward, easy-to-use way. They don't overpromise and, as a result, don't underdeliver. The experience is consistent and uniform; I may not be excited to be flying them, but I'm not disappointed, either. No hassles, no headache.

One of the most interesting stories percolating in commercial aviation right now is that of Turkish Airlines and its plan to emulate the success of Emirates over the next five years. More than a few aviation analysts have found these plans audacious and amusing. Turkish Airlines is a relatively obscure carrier in the States, and Emirates is the third largest airline in the world, despite operating for less than twenty years and having little to work with at first.[4] Indeed, when they launched, there weren't any obvious benefits for travelers who chose to book with them instead of established Western carriers. Pre-celebrity Dubai offered few reasons for foreigners to fly to the city.

If Emirates was going to create a product that was viewed as superior to existing carriers, they needed to do two things: First, they had to find a way to reduce the perception of transiting through Dubai as a hassle, and then they had to simultaneously create the impression that their flight experience offered meaningful benefits to passengers. Emirates figured that the *What* they could offer was a fantastic connection point for passengers looking to get from one side of the planet to the other. They added a reputation for ultra-high-end luxury in first and business class, emphasized the newly glitzy Westernized Dubai, bought the newest aircraft available, and implemented hiring practices that emphasized youth and beauty in their flight attendants. They squeezed an extra seat (and extra revenue) in each economy row of their workhorse 777s (ten across, as compared to American Airlines' nine), but placated their cramped economy passengers with good food and fantastic in-flight entertainment. Most important, they allowed travelers to trade painfully overcrowded hubs like Heathrow and Charles de Gaulle for brand-new, and highly efficient, transit experiences at Dubai. Their popularity has dealt them one serious disadvantage: None of the major airline alliances want to partner with them. However, even mileage-hungry businesspeople are willing to accept the tradeoff of nontransferable frequent-flyer miles and go with Emirates, precisely because it eliminated some of the hassles that they'd been accustomed to experiencing while flying.[5]

Emirates has successfully circumvented their own limitations, at least for now. They've designed strategies that offer a perceived benefit to travelers who might otherwise choose less luxurious and less modern American or British carriers. They've figured out their *What*, and it appears to be working. The government-owned airline claims to have made a profit nearly every year it's been in operation.

Who knows if Turkish Airlines can copy the success of Emirates' *What*. Istanbul's location on the border of the Eastern and Western worlds offers a similar transit advantage for global passengers. The airline is working hard to elevate passengers' onboard experience and is lobbying the government for a third Istanbul airport. The airline planners were clever to place aircraft orders just as the aviation industry was bottoming out. Their current advertising campaign features global sports stars like players from Manchester United and Kobe Bryant relaxing in Turkish Airlines' new first- and business-class seats.[6] Hopefully, the management team is doing more than simply aiming to replicate Emirates' success, and will devise a strategy that offers their own unique benefits to customers. We'll see.

SPARKING POINTS

- What hassles would I need to overcome for my customers in order to leapfrog over my competitors' product?
- What would I need to do differently?
- How will our competitors respond to these changes?

What features of my product create unanticipated passion?

What would you have to do to make your company, and its product, so essential to your customer that they would refuse to let your business die? Imagine that kind of passion for what you do. Imagine a customer base so emotionally invested in the unique characteristics and qualities of your particular brand that they will take on the huge technical challenge of keeping your product alive, long after common sense—and your board—declares it should die. This is exactly what the Impossible Project is currently doing with Polaroid Company's instant film division. In 2008, two men—one of them a long time Polaroid employee, the other a committed fan of analog photography—heard the news that Polaroid was ceasing production of their classic instant film packs. The two men decided to be bold and do something seemingly foolish. They bought the relevant machinery from Polaroid, leased the plant, and rounded up a core group of employees who'd worked in the instant film division. They then set about essentially re-creating the instant film product from scratch. On a rational level, Polaroid film is an obsolete product that has run its course. But on an emotional level it's a "warm" product, which means that it is something that a substantial number of fans have a deeply emotional, rather than logical, connection to. Need proof? Just look at your home page on Facebook; if it's anything like mine, you can easily scroll through pages of smartphone Hipstamatic photographs. These digital versions of an analog experience take an unexceptional photograph and saturate it with the flaws, bleached-out or oversaturated colors, and slight distortions that came with the original Polaroid experience.

You could argue that Polaroid was reacting pragmatically and logically to the fundamental change from film to digital photography. Most professional photographers no longer wanted an instant film test of a setup that they were going to shoot digitally. Families and individuals were making the same transition in their home photography. Continuing to produce an obsolete product is foolishness. However, what the Impossible Project was able to do is isolate the elements of the instant film business that still had value, emphasize them, and promote them to exactly the people who would recognize, appreciate, and pay for those values.

Impossible Project film comes at a premium price of up to three dollars per exposure. They are open about the fact that the films and the dyes used in them are still experimental in nature, and offer unpredictable results. Their film won't deliver lifelike colors, and the end results vary depending on the temperature at which they are shot. Using their film is a test of a photographer's skill and creativity. In other words, they've stripped out the predictability and ease of use that was Polaroid's original selling point to the mainstream masses. In their place they've ratcheted up the elements that matter to people who are truly passionate about Polaroid: its malleability, its subtle tones and colors, and the special effects that can be created if you manipulate the dyes before they have finished processing. It takes a good eye, quick reactions, and skill to get a great result from the new film, which adds up to one major selling point for the Impossible Project. If you grew up in the '70s, '80s, or '90s, and were at all "artsy," you probably cut a fresh Polaroid in half and used the wet emulsion to create a reverse image in your journal. Now your kids can have the same experience, albeit for three times the price.

Polaroid's decision to shutter their instant-film plant may have been the right one for them. The Impossible Project garners huge amounts of press, but their sales are still modest, and certainly insufficient to have kept the original Polaroid business model going. However, it's surprising that Polaroid was unable to understand, or leverage, their customers' love for their product into *something*.

An emotional bond with your customer is essential to creating a "must-have" product. It's tempting to think that this link only happens organically, but you can forge this connection in a strategic manner. The Sparking Points below will get you thinking about the value of forging this bond, ways of doing it, and how to fully leverage the bond once it's in place.

SPARKING POINTS

- What are the features that have elicited the strongest emotional response from your customers?
- How do you ensure these are carried forward both in your current and future products?
- How do you avoid killing the passion?

What emotional, psychological, or status benefits could people derive from using my product?

Do you have diamonds stashed away that you reckon you can sell if times ever get tough? Say, a family heirloom, or an engagement ring from a failed marriage? Perhaps you know how much the diamond was appraised for by a reputable seller and feel confident that you can get a reasonable return on your investment. If so, you're in for a disappointing surprise.[7]

In the late 1880s, a group of British financiers who'd invested heavily in South African diamond mines grew alarmed at the discovery of vast new supplies of the supposedly scarce gem. They realized that the value of their *What*—diamonds—was essentially the public's perception of them as both extremely rare (and thus valuable), and a sign of sophistication and affluence. This belief about what the diamond merchants were selling would be irreparably damaged if the world's markets were suddenly flooded with the gems. The financiers banded together, formed the De Beers consortium, and have managed and manipulated both the supply of diamonds and the public's perception of them ever since. In the late 1940s, they coined the phrase "A diamond is forever" and persuaded young couples everywhere that the purchase of one was an essential symbol of love and devotion. In the late '50s, they responded to a glut of tiny diamonds from the Soviet Union by creating the idea of and the market for the "eternity ring." The eternity ring was promoted as a gift for established couples to celebrate their ongoing commitment. Rather than one large diamond, the ring was comprised of a string of tiny diamonds set in a band. Prior to the eternity ring, customers were more interested in purchasing large diamonds. De Beers was able to convince consumers that these small diamonds were equally desirable by creating the idea that the small diamonds represented the passing of the years.[8] Smart. Even more cleverly, they realized that by marketing diamonds as both investments and emotional signifiers, customers would keep them rather than reselling them down the line. You might part with Grandma's bond portfolio, but you were far less likely to sell her ring. This sentiment helps keep untold billions of dollars of privately owned diamonds off of the market, thereby keeping the price of "new" diamonds high. Brilliant.

However, the actual value of a diamond is negligible. Recently, a friend took a loose diamond to a dealer. She had vague plans of buying a twin for it and making earrings for her daughter. The dealer squinted at the stone for a moment and quoted her $7,000 for a diamond that would match. When she balked, he looked up at her, and without blinking an eye, offered to buy *her* stone for $2,000. She politely declined.

The diamond industry has expertly shepherded their customers into thinking and believing certain things about their product. Now, I'm not necessarily advocating this kind of strategic manipulation, but it's interesting to look at how flexibly and fluidly De Beers is able to revise what their product actually is. By doing this, they are able to reflect the realities of the existing marketplace and also create markets where there were none.

De Beers has answered this Killer Question, most recently with the creation of the "right-hand ring." It was first unveiled in the early 2000s as the luxury goods market was nearing its apex. The right-hand ring is, like most engagement rings, made of diamonds and set in platinum. However, unlike an engagement ring, it is made for women to buy for themselves, as a symbol of emancipation and self-worth.[9]

I would have loved to have sat in on the concept meetings for the right-hand ring. The diamond industry has been very clever in adjusting their product to both lead and respond to social changes, and I'm sure the right-hand ring is no different. The ring hit at a moment when the consumption of big-ticket luxury items felt like a statement of success and self-acceptance. It was a clever idea that subverted what buying a diamond ring traditionally means, turning it from a symbol of commitment and marriage into a declaration of independence and freedom. The diamond industry has managed to create two products that are basically the same thing, yet fine-tune two completely different messages for them and thus create two different markets. At the same time, there is no public sense of a contradiction between them, and thus they've been able to add a whole new audience without compromising their existing one.

There is something pretty clever about the way the diamond industry has both manipulated existing markets and created new ones. Their products are imbued with both emotional value and the perception of "real" value. Owners feel that the diamonds convey a sense of wealth and prosperity, even though the stones are nearly always worth dramatically less than the owners believe. There are also larger questions about the way diamonds are obtained from the third world. However, no one can deny that the marketing minds of De Beers have done a fantastic job at both shaping their customers' needs and criteria and responding to them.

SPARKING POINTS

- Does your product create a connection with its consumer that goes beyond just being a good solution to their needs?
- Can you refine it to reflect the changing needs and desires of your customer?
- Is the emotional connection literally between the customer and the product, or between the customer and what the product signifies to them?
- Are there good or interesting reasons to resist an emotional connection and actively prevent one from developing?

Can I create an on-demand version of the product?

Do you need to have a finished product in order to make a sale? Is there any way that *not* offering a finished product would actually give you an advantage, or even become a selling point? Suppose that your manufacturing costs appear to have gotten as low as they can without sacrificing quality. Even if your costs are acceptable to you, you still have to deal with the lag time between ordering a product and having it manufactured and shipped to you—typically six weeks from China. Perhaps this lag time causes you to lose sales, or to miss the window of opportunity for your product if you're aiming to respond quickly to a short-lived fad. Is there any other option besides relying on this manufacturing and supply chain?

My children have long since outgrown toys, but if they were still young today, I'd probably be roped into visits to Build-A-Bear. Build-A-Bear, like the paint-your-own pottery craze that preceded it, doesn't offer a finished product. In fact, the whole selling point is that you create your own customized product in-store. These types of businesses are offering a dual product: both the end result—be it a stuffed animal in a personalized costume or an "I Love Dad" coffee mug—and the chance to create something without taking responsibility for gathering materials or cleaning up the mess it generates. A stuffed toy may feel like a low-risk product, but children's tastes, interests, and fads can be as fickle as an adult's. Just ask any parent. Once you start adding the layers of design and complexity to a toy—clothes, accessories, prerecorded sounds—you risk creating something that misses the mark with your target audience. Build-A-Bear's strategy is very clever in that it allows them to keep components, rather than finished products, as inventory. They never have to run the risk of being stuck with 10,000 astronaut bears the week after the latest *Pirates of the Caribbean* opens. Or conversely, having 10,000 pirate bears in anticipation of a hit, only to find the franchise has run out of gas and the kids don't care.

There are two points to take from this. The first is that these companies are reducing their risk of having a stockroom full of faddish, briefly popular products that they now can't sell. The second is that they are able to charge their customers a premium for the pleasure of assembling the final bear. They've been able to persuade their customers that down is up. They don't offer a fully finished product for sale, and if you *do* want their product, you'll have to assemble it yourself.

Genius.

Home bakers have experienced a similar shift in how they "make" a product—for example, a cake. When I was a kid, my grandma would make me a cake from scratch every year. The cake cost maybe a dollar in commodity goods. When she passed away, my mom took over the job. She'd buy a cake mix, add an egg, some oil, and some water, and that was it. Of course, the cake was more expensive because of the convenience factor of having pre-made cake mix. When I was eight, my mom got a job as a Realtor and had no time to bake, so she'd order a cake, which was probably twenty-five dollars, for the even greater convenience factor.

These days, if you have young kids, a cake—either homemade or store-bought—no longer cuts it. Instead, you are paying hundreds of dollars for a party in an ice-cream store. There's a relationship here between the amount you're paying and the experience you're receiving.[10] Selling these products is about more than simple convenience. Manufacturers have to walk a thin line between making a product so easy that it feels like cheating, and so complex that the user sees no value in the supposed "convenience." When cake mixes first came out, they were really simple; all you had to do was add water. But women didn't like it, because it felt too easy—like they hadn't contributed anything to it, and couldn't claim any pride in making it. So cake mixes were altered to require a fresh egg as well, and the product took off.

The Pillsbury Doughboy ads played on this same idea. Their sales pitch is less about the superior taste or ingredients than it is about allowing Mom the satisfaction of putting hand-baked rolls in front of her family. Same with Sandra Lee's *Semi-Homemade* TV show. Both of these brands allow their users to bypass any guilt they might feel at not being able to offer their family the full experience of a homemade meal. The users get the pleasure of the last step: pulling something hot and fresh out of the oven and serving it to their family.

If you want to build this kind of emotional connection with your customer, you need to look at how you can offer them a creative "I did this" kind of experience. You want to give your customer a chance to feel like they've done something special for their family or loved ones by making something for them. There's also a positive customer experience in being able to feel a sense of personal pride in something they've done for themselves. Can you give them an opportunity to take ownership over the construction process?

Look at ways in which you can add real value for your customer while simultaneously giving them a less-finished product that improves your bottom line or supply and manufacturing protocol.

Can you give them the chance to say "I did this"?

SPARKING POINTS

- What benefits would you get if you were able to sell your product such that the customer assembles it?
- Could assembling it be pitched as a learning, bonding, or more authentic process?
- Could you increase the perceived value, and hence the cost, of your product by emphasizing its real-time availability?

Can I recombine existing components to create new products for customers I don't currently serve?

Magazine publishers are in the same predicament as the book-publishing and recording industries before it. How do you keep your customers believing that your content is worth paying for when there is endless free content available on the Internet? Some fashion magazines are experimenting with making their print issues feel like "must-buy" items; *Bazaar* and *Elle* both offer subscriber-only covers with edgier photography. Others, like the British style magazine *i-D*, routinely print magazines with multiple, collectible covers. There is a growing audience for boutique fashion magazines that have high cover prices and only come out once or twice a year, making them less like magazines and more like very fashionable books.

Other magazine publishers are looking at ways to monetize their "back catalogue" of content. Condé Nast has an app that creates a customizable city guide for readers. The content on this app is based on existing articles.[11] For instance, if you're planning a vacation to Italy, you'll get travel tips from *Condé Nast Traveler*, recipes to inspire you from *Bon Appétit*, fashion stories from *Vogue*, and lists of important buildings to see from *Architectural Digest*.

Magazine publishers think of their assets as magazine titles, when in reality, their assets are the tens of thousands of articles that have been written over the years and published in titles like *Traveler*. So, how do they continue to extract value from these old assets? Does your business have an equivalent backlog of information or experience that you could reshape into a current product?

Condé Nast is a rare example of a publishing company that is actively looking to extract value from their back catalogue. Most publishers are still stuck in their old ways of how they've always done things. Those that are willing to experiment and try this repurposing will be the ones to discover new areas of growth for their business. It's not a question of change happening ten years from now. The revolution in magazine media is happening today, and choosing not to participate is just foolish.

As is often the case, it is the people and companies who are in trouble, and fighting for survival, who are the boldest. Sometimes desperation is the key to getting you out of a rut. The first magazine to offer an iPad app wasn't *Time* or *Vogue* but *Interview,* which is a struggling and somewhat avant-garde NYC culture magazine.[12] The people who feel the cliff crumbling beneath their feet the fastest often have a boldness that their more secure competitors lack. If everything seems like it's going to fall away beneath you, you have less to lose, and you're empowered to make riskier, but possibly life-saving, moves. I don't know if a magazine app will save *Interview,* but the fact they are trying demonstrates their willingness to evolve and fight for their survival.

SPARKING POINTS

- Are you making the assumption that your product needs to be sold as a whole, single unit, simply because that's how the manufacturing and distribution model works today?
- Could you provide your product components as individual pieces or in unique combinations? What new customers could you serve?
- What changes would this require in your business model?

Who will not buy my product because they feel something is objectionable about it?

The flipside to any positive emotional connotation or connection is a negative one. If you are inspiring enough such that some people *love* what you are doing, odds are you are going to be inspiring others to *dislike* your product with an equal passion. Plenty of companies trade on the fact that they represent something the mainstream culture will find offensive or questionable. Look at any business that sells rebellion or a gritty countercultural message. Even more mainstream products such as those found in the tobacco or alcohol industries subtly sell themselves as being a little dangerous and outside the norm. The question for you is to decide whether there is any benefit or purpose to being strategically *disliked* or being perceived by some as "not us." Will it benefit you and your product to deliberately set yourself in opposition to certain social groups? And if so, how do you accomplish this? This strategy can be positive if it allows you to clearly define what you are about and who you are targeting. The important thing is to carefully walk the line between creating connection on one side and provoking rejection on the other.

Look at the growing trend of restaurants and gastropubs that refuse to offer any substitutions on their menu. Father's Office in L.A.'s Culver City has great burgers, but only serves them one way: with caramelized onions, bacon, gruyère, blue cheese, and arugula—no ketchup. If you want ketchup, you'll have to sneak in your own packets and be careful that the waitstaff doesn't catch you using them. You'd think that a restaurant with this kind of draconian policy against customization would be dead in the water. Not so. If you want to eat at Father's Office, you'll be waiting hours for a table; it's packed, day and night. Some people hate Father's Office, and I have friends in L.A. who flatout refuse to set foot in the place. That's fine. The people who love it really, really love it—both for the food and for its slightly contrarian atmosphere. The negative emotional response it provokes in other people only solidifies the fans' passion for the place.

SPARKING POINTS

- Have you ever tried to market your product based on what it doesn't supply rather than on what it does?
- Can you use the thing that's objectionable about your product to create a community of customers?
- How could eliminating the objection help or hurt you?

What is surprisingly inconvenient about my product?

The designers and engineers who work at HP face many challenges in getting their ideas signed off on. It's a long process from an idea to a finished prototype. Before any product can hit the market, it faced one final test. I would take the prototype home, give it to my wife, and say, "Tell me what you think."[13] Now, my wife is an extremely smart and focused individual, but she is emphatically not a techie. She doesn't care *how* a gadget works; she just wants it to *work*.

Her lack of specialized knowledge has been hugely valuable to me over the years. If I test a new product, I can troubleshoot it almost without thinking. I might not even notice a glitch that could cause major hassles for an end consumer because the fix is second-nature to me. On the other hand, if my wife can't get a product to work, the first thing she does is call me up and yell at me, which is a great incentive to get our products as flawless as possible.

Several years ago, she was relocating her stained-glass studio to California from our former home on the East Coast. She was a little nervous about the drive. Luckily, HP was working on the the first working model for the latest GPS device. The team wanted her to test it, so I gave her a quick lesson, and off she went. Three days later, she calls me from the road, almost speechless with rage. The device looked great and had the latest hardware features anyone could want. What it didn't have was accurate maps. Every time my wife searched for something, it came up empty.

When she finally made it out west, she met me for lunch at the HP cafeteria. The team that had given her the device came up and asked her what she thought. Her response? "Well, it was clearly designed by a guy; I stopped at every crummy gas-station bathroom between here and Kentucky!" The GPS was super fast, looked great, but had completely missed the mark on why people buy GPS devices, which is based almost purely on the quality of the maps and points of interest like highway rest-stops. Great hardware can't compensate for faulty software.[14]

The GPS device failed the wife test.

There are two ways to uncover these kinds of potential annoyances in your new or existing products. One is to observe your customers and see what they are doing with your product and what their experience with it is. The other is, use the product yourself. Either way, you need to be fanatical about constantly improving the product and getting rid of the problems you uncover. Keep in mind that I've observed major differences between how men and women handle these issues. Guys have ego wrapped up in their new devices; they won't let the gadget win. A woman will give it three chances; if she tries to use a new product three times and it doesn't work, she'll take it back to the store because she doesn't have any interest in fighting with the product and *winning*. Men are much more likely to keep tinkering with the device and, if all else fails, stick it in the garage and forget about it. If it doesn't work for a woman, she'll let you know, and you'll have a returned product on your store shelves. This is one of the reasons I rely so heavily on the wife test; my wife is a zero-tolerance consumer. If you don't have a zero-tolerance consumer, you need to find one and embrace them. Have them test your products and give you the unvarnished truth about your products' real usefulness and value.

SPARKING POINTS

- How do you uncover what customers perceive to be inconvenient about your product? Are you aware of the inconveniences?
- Do you use your own product or service?
- What's your version of the wife test?

What products could I create out of unused assets?

I'm an innovation guy. It may not say so on my business card, but that's what I do. I encourage people, whether inside HP or in my meetings with customers around the world, to accept that they and their product are going to have to change. No matter how popular and successful your work is, things change. The economy shifts; your customers' needs evolve; technologies become redundant. We've talked about this in earlier chapters, but looking forward, preparing for the inevitable evolutions in your business and your product, is crucial if you're going to succeed.

Amazon has been brilliant at refining *What* they do and *How* they do it to reflect the changing criteria of *Who* they're doing it for. This kind of flexibility is to be expected in the formative and pliable early years of a business or industry. What's impressive is that Amazon has retained that spirit even as they've solidified into the cornerstone of the digital marketplace.

The first phase of the Amazon era addressed readers' criteria and hassles in the mid-'90s. They made it easy to buy any book, no matter how niche or obscure, thereby undercutting Borders and Barnes & Noble to offer a cheaper product, and saving you a trip to the mall in the process. Mission accomplished. This very simple *What*—cheaper books, huge selection, delivered to your door—worked. Since then, they've diversified the products offered to the point where they are essentially an online department store. They've experimented with everything from a search engine—A9 (built on the Google platform, but not a hit)—to allowing small booksellers a chance to list their books on the site.[15] Their Amazon Mechanical Turk service allows individuals to make money by offering their services in tiny increments of time. Have five minutes free? Make a little money transcribing a two-minute podcast.

Whether any of these *What*s are really a good idea is up for debate. Amazon's detractors argue that they are diluting their core message and product. I'd counter that they are taking risks and exploring new uses for their existing infrastructure. Many of Amazon's explorations in creating new value are based around a tweak of this Killer Question, which goes something like "Is there unused space in my existing infrastructure that could be filled?"

Amazon has vastly more server capacity than they generally need in order to address requirements at peak times such as the Christmas holiday season or Black Friday. As a result, they have taken their cue from companies like Rackspace and Media Temple and have begun renting their servers to provide infrastructure for third-party websites. Their leap from selling books and other retail goods to getting into the computing infrastructure business has been unexpected. But it has worked well. Amazon S3 is very successful, and lots of start-ups use it.[16] As long as you have a credit card number, you can have servers and storage. Amazon can easily allocate you more space on the servers as your business grows and needs more capacity.

The lesson here is to avoid being pigeonholed into one set of services. Take a look at any underused resources you have available. Is there a way that you could offer these to your customers as an auxiliary service to your main business?

Finding ways to offer underused resources as a service and see income where there would otherwise be none is brilliant. These explorations might not yield big payoffs, but the point is that you need to be constantly looking at new ways to stay ahead of the trends that are shaping your industry.

SPARKING POINTS

- Are there year-round or seasonally based un- or underused assets or capabilities in your company (real estate, capacity, distribution, etc.)?
- What customers, partners, or suppliers could benefit from having access to those assets?
- What business model would you need in order to promote, sell, or support a set of products or services around these unused assets?

YOUR FUTURE WHAT

I don't know how the business world is going to evolve. All I know for sure is that it *is* going to evolve, and that the pace of this evolution is going to get faster than we can imagine now. Think about music and ask yourself: What's a song? What should a music fan expect to experience when they listen to an album?

Late last year, HP was developing a laptop that would deliver the highest-quality audio ever achieved on a PC. It's amazing stuff. This was game-changing enough to have a steady stream of cutting-edge recording artists coming through our California facilities to hear about it and try it out. One of those artists who I was lucky enough to get a little time with was Will.i.am.

I know nothing about the Black Eyed Peas. My kids are fans, but not the tech guys I meet in my usual life. Still, I figured I'd meet and greet, get in a few moments with an important cultural figure, and be on my way. Three hours later, we were still deep in conversation. Will.i.am blew me away; he sees no boundaries to what music can be, or how it should be heard. I can't share the innovations he's working on, but let's just say Will.i.am *asks questions*. He wants to know *why* every listener has to hear an album track in the same way. *Why* can't the listener experience a customized track—almost like a live concert— each time they listen to a song? *Why* do we still experience music as a complete, finished product in essentially the same way our great-grandparents did with their phonograph?

I have no idea whether Will.i.am's current preoccupation with changing how we experience music will take. Maybe people don't want music to be fluid and changeable; maybe making a song customizable would strip its potential for becoming an iconic anthem. Who knows? I don't. All I do know is that Will.i.am is asking questions, refusing to accept the assumptions of his industry, and moving forward even as his peers relax in their successes or struggle with their failures. One day he'll come up with something that will change the way we experience many, and perhaps all, forms of entertainment and information. And that's amazing.

What products and services will I need to develop and offer to stay ahead of my competition in the next five years?

On October 4, 1957, Russia launched a beach-ball-sized satellite named *Sputnik,* which orbited the Earth in just over ninety-six minutes. The previous frontrunner in the space race, the United States, was now the runner-up. Our only competitor had trounced us, seemingly out of nowhere. A month later, the Russians sent up Laika, a small stray terrier collected from the streets of Moscow, in *Sputnik II.* The dog became the first living creature sent into space, and an instant celebrity back on Earth.

The "*Sputnik* moment" ended up being a huge benefit for our long-term space goals. The US government was shocked and embarrassed that Soviet Russia managed to beat us into space. In 1958, NASA was founded, and a few years later President Kennedy greatly increased funding for space travel. The United States led the way for the next half century.[17]

We all need *Sputnik* moments. Yes, they can be alarming, but they are also invigorating. A *Sputnik* moment is the catalyst for change because seeing your enemy get ahead is the greatest motivator there is. It makes you see that you have to seriously improve your game if you want to win. A *Sputnik* moment makes you realize that if you don't change, you're going to get left behind—and soon. Have you ever had a *Sputnik* moment?

SPARKING POINTS

- What future predictions can you make based on the innovation rate for your industry (e.g., Moore's law in the computer industry)?
- What decisions would you make today if you knew that the rate of innovation would double in the next three to five years?
- What "impossible" idea (product, service, solution) have you been ignoring because it can't happen? What would need to be done to make it happen?

How could my product change in five years?

Do you sell atoms or bits? Do you think that your answer could change over the next five years? Think about Amazon and the Kindle. Jeff Bezos asked, *What is my role going to be if the nature of books changes?* He realized that to stay relevant and necessary his company needed to retain control over something tangible and physical. There could have been other options. Amazon could have bet that the reading experience would fully transition to audio, but they ultimately gambled that the act of reading was still integral to the enjoyment of a book. So, how do you stay in control of a physical experience when your product is going from atoms to bits?

Think about what a profound change this is. What would you do if your physical product—one that has been around, unchanged, for hundreds or thousands of years—suddenly seemed headed toward obsolescence? How do you still keep yourself relevant—an essential part of a transaction or an experience—especially if, like Amazon, you are primarily functioning as the middleman between product and customer? How do you keep that link alive?

For Amazon, that link is providing the medium that brings the printed word to the reader. First, that medium was books, and now, for many, it's the Kindle. Amazon has been smart to keep physical ownership over the process of reading. Even though a reader may have transferred allegiance to digital media, Amazon is *still controlling access to the "thing" in a reader's hand*. Granted, there are plenty of competitors springing up, all with their own pros and cons, but none has both the sheer heft of Amazon's catalogue and the huge advantage of having arrived so early on the market. A Kindle, like the Hoover vacuum cleaner before it, is becoming both the specific name of the product, and a catch-all term for its category—a great place to be.

It will be interesting to see how far Amazon pushes the possibilities of the Kindle, and how its relationships with publishers and authors will develop. Publishers are no longer in the business of selling paper, yet most still act as though they are. The publishing industry is still figuring out exactly how to handle pricing on e-books, and especially how e-book pricing can be aligned with traditional book pricing in a way that makes sense to the consumer. Customers are not happy to pay more for a Kindle edition than a hardcover edition of a bestseller. Yet some books are more expensive as digital downloads than as hardcovers. It doesn't make sense to consumers, and it's a downright dangerous situation for all concerned if book piracy takes off in the same way that music piracy did a decade ago. You don't want to antagonize your customers or make them feel like fools for buying what you are selling. Offering a digital download for more than a hardcover does just that.

SPARKING POINTS

- What societal, economic, and demographic changes will affect your customers over the next five years?
- Are you missing weak signals about the future of your industry because you feel like the seismic shifts will not affect you?

What Comes Next?

A few years ago, I saw a website offering a product called After the Rapture Pet Care. It claimed to offer a service for Christians concerned about the welfare of pets that would be left behind after the Day of Judgment. Subscribers were promised a network of non-Christians who'd swoop in, collect pets, and promise to care for them and tend to their needs in the absence of their owners. I'm not sure if this was a parody or not. My suspicion is that, even if it were offered as a sincere business, the owners had no expectation of ever needing to make good on their service. Still, it makes a point. The only boundary to the innovation and development of a new product—a *What*—is your willingness to get out there, think up an idea, no matter how crazy, and give it a shot. Venture capital is a great thing, but if you're sitting there telling yourself you *can't* do something, can't get your *What* out there because of a lack of cash, time, expertise, etc., then you're missing the point. Success has always been part inspiration, part ideation, and part tenacity. Don't put yourself in the position of seeing someone else make your idea happen. Don't be that person sitting in a bar, telling everyone within earshot about how *you had that idea first*. It doesn't matter if you had that idea first; it matters if you made it happen first.

CHAPTER 8

How *It Gets Done*

When I first started to write the Killer Questions, I needed a structure to bind them together into a program that I could share or teach. I quickly realized that asking Killer Questions about *What* and *Who* was obvious. You need to know *what you are creating*, and *whom you are creating it for*. *How* you do this is subtler. *How* stitches together *What* you are doing, and *Who* you are doing it for. It is literally *how* you deliver value to your customer with your product.

You can have a great idea, and a potential customer base of people who need and want it, but before you can get to the end result—a successful sale and ongoing relationship with your client—you need to understand the processes and strategies that come between the moment your product is first conceived of, and the moment a customer "rewards" your final product by purchasing it. The Killer Questions in this chapter are focused on the continual development and evolution of the processes you have in place to deliver value to your customer. Whether you oversee a multinational corporation or run a one-person operation out of your garage, your business lives and dies by how your organization operates. By the end of this chapter, I hope you'll have used the questions to understand how you, your product, your employees, and the marketplace are all linked together, and how, like any chain, you are only as strong as your weakest link.

IIIIIIIIIIIIII

The online shopping boom and bubble of the '90s was all about changing the process of distribution, and this change has influenced how millions of people buy books, clothes, music, and just about everything. Cyber Monday is as meaningful a shopping event as Black Friday, with sales of more than one billion dollars in 2010.[1] However, the Internet shopping phenomenon took time to solidify. In the late '90s, plenty of visionaries saw that by bypassing brick-and-mortar and going "virtual only," they could make huge profits in online retailing. Yet most failed to ask the fundamental Killer Questions of how exactly they would do this. While the Internet meltdown of the '90s has been well documented, it's worth pulling out a few key examples from that era.

Anyone remember Boo.com? Back in 1999, they were going to change the way the world bought sportswear. Run by three young Swedes, Boo.com hired a large international staff. Their global offices took top-of-the-line real estate in London, New York, and Paris. They spent millions hiring a huge staff, building a complex infrastructure, and developing "Miss Boo," an animated interactive shopping assistant to guide customers through their sneaker purchases. They ran a hip marketing campaign in the United States and Europe. Shortly before their big launch, they ran a trial sales day, open to the friends and family of staff members. By the end of the day, the sales figures trickled in. Italy's tally? One key chain, which was later returned. What happened? Among many problems were some absurdly simple ones: The average customer's computer was too slow to run Miss Boo, or the groundbreaking rotational viewpoints of the available products. The website was not compatible with Mac, yet a large segment of the urban hipsters the company targeted were Mac users. Further, for those customers who could access the site, the unique user interface was too slow and constantly crashed. Customers who wanted to make purchases grew frustrated and gave up. If they could make it to the content pages, they found products that were surprisingly bland and poorly curated. Despite the fiercely hip image that Boo.com projected, as well as a prominent story in *Vogue*, most of the actual sneakers and sports clothing they sold were easily available in high-street stores. There was no compelling reason to go through the hoops of shopping on Boo, so customers gave up trying.[2, 3]

The point of this story isn't to single out one of the many Internet start-ups that crashed and burned in spectacular fashion. Instead, I want to contrast this with the way Amazon.com kept their business model lean and simple. Jeff Bezos and his team enabled their customer to browse and find books, order them, and have them show up without the hassle of getting in the car. Their *How* worked, perfectly. Boo put their focus on a flashy exterior, and never really thought about how their site would serve their customers' needs.

Boo seemed to feel that the *experience* of using their site offered some kind of value to the customer. It was cutting-edge, hip. It appealed to users' desire to be insiders. Yet companies like Boo flopped because they failed across a number of the metrics that they used to operate their business. Did they really understand how to bring value to their customers? Were they really thinking of their customers when they chose to emphasize flashy and sophisticated presentation over price, convenience, and simplicity?

Timing Is Everything

I am a huge believer in the importance of timing, and it's critically important in the process of developing and bringing innovation to market. When you're looking at a failure like Boo, keep in mind that the fundamental idea might have been sound, but that it might have faltered simply because the resources necessary to make the *How* work were not yet in place. There are obvious dangers in bringing a product to market too late, but there are equal dangers in being too early. Introducing a product into the marketplace at the right time is a crucial *How* skill. Knowing the difference between a product that will work eventually and one that is doomed to fail no matter when it enters the market is a second and equally critical skill.

What is the first company you think of when you think of snap-shots and home photography? It's probably Kodak. Now look at your digital camera. It isn't a Kodak, is it? Did you know that Kodak actually developed one of the first commercially available digital cameras in the early '90s? The DC40 was big, expensive, and could store a maximum of 96 photographs at a low-quality setting. Users would download the photos via cable to their computer. Kodak pushed their digital cameras hard. Successive models that could hold more images at higher resolutions followed the DC40. Kodak discovered that women in particular loved taking digital photographs, but hated the difficulties of downloading them onto the computer. So Kodak invented the printer dock, which allowed photos to be directly printed from the camera. However, as hard as Kodak pushed, they were never able to get ahead of the digital game. They had a first-mover advantage, and the ideas were good, but the timing was off. Kodak felt they could go it alone rather than expand the value chain with outside companies or suppliers (at one time in their history, they even had their own herds of cattle to supply gelatin for their film stock). Other, nimbler companies were able to react more quickly to the changes in technology and customer needs. Even when Kodak kept up, they struggled to deal with the huge decrease in profits that came in their core business as people stopped buying, developing, and printing film.[4]

Kodak's leadership had incredible foresight to realize that the film era was on its way out and to pursue a huge investment in digital photography. Yet they were also victims of their vision. They debuted an innovative technology that the market was not yet ready to embrace. When that product didn't take off, they used its failure as an excuse to adopt the point of view that their customer did not really want digital, and that their existing film business was not at risk. This is a great example of Clayton Christensen's "innovator's dilemma," where the first generation of a radical new innovation is rejected because the company believes that it's not as good as the current generation (in this case, film).[5] It's a basic but convincing rationalization to keep on doing what you are doing. If Kodak had avoided the innovator's dilemma and focused on the long-term vision that the market was changing, they could have (eventually) won.

If you let yourself be lulled into a comfortable place by the failure of a bold change, then you're going to find yourself in trouble. If the lion's share of your revenue is coming from your existing business, it can be incredibly hard to walk the line between change and the status quo, especially if you're looking at radical innovations. A truly radical change, such as the transition from film to digital, can mean that your new business is going to destroy your old. If you don't attack your core business, your competition will. This is one of the hardest things for management teams to do. How do you go after your core business? How do you deal with the reality that you need to destroy it, or at least render it obsolete, to stay ahead as a company? This is what happened to Kodak; they sensed that they needed to kill film with something game-changing if they wanted to stay on top, but they couldn't quite get there. In the end, their competitors killed their core business for them, and they've been struggling to regain their footing ever since.

Kodak is a good example of the dangers of being so comfortable and set in your ways that you are completely unprepared to act. Kodak needed to seek outside ideas and bring them into their products in order to survive. If they had been willing to ask some tough, painful *How* questions, they would have sensed the urgency of the moment and realized how critically important the choices they were making were.

Delivering Value to Your Customers

What do you think of when you think about the innovation process? Where do you think you can bring new ideas and new philosophies to your company? Is it a new product? Or a new group of customers that you've never thought about approaching before? These are both smart and obvious places to bring change and innovation into your business (and are covered in chapters 7 and 6, respectively). However, if you limit yourself to thinking about your product and your customer, you are missing a third of the puzzle—namely, the way you create and deliver: the *How*.

The *How* chapter is structured around the value chain, a set of processes that encompasses everything that goes on behind the scenes in order to deliver the value of your product to your customer. It is easy to get complacent about *How* you do things. Your value chain is less glamorous and can seem less interesting than the process of creating a great product. However, if your competitors are equally complacent about constantly reviewing (and if necessary, revising) the way they do things, then you have an advantage. You'll have a way to get ahead by simply innovating new ways of organizing your marketing/advertising, sales teams, supply chain, or manufacturing and distribution of your product. Remember, there needs to be only one competitor who comes up with a radical innovation, and you're in the dust.

And don't make the mistake of thinking you can outsource these kind of insights. My skin crawls when I hear that a company has brought in an outside analyst to help them implement best practices. Best practices are, by definition, the industry standard. In other words, average . . . and who wants to be average? Think of the scene in *The Incredibles* where Dash's mom tells him that everyone's special. Dash responds by muttering to himself, "which is another way of saying no one is."

So what is getting in the way of you having *How* insights by yourself? We all have blind spots about how we operate as individuals and work as part of a team. In order to move forward, you need to be able to see and work around them. Blind spots are, essentially, the "obvious answers" that are based on what we did or didn't do in the past, what we learned in school, and what we have seen work for others. They can be about our individual strengths and weaknesses, or they can be about the very nature of our business and the role it fills in the marketplace.

It's easy to talk about avoiding blind spots by innovating all of the elements in your value chain. It's harder to actually sit down and consider changing the way you do things. I know, because I've done it, or observed it being done, many times. A few years ago, HP made some major innovations in how we purchased the components that went into the products we sell. As part of this effort, we tasked a team of researchers in HP Labs to radically revise the mathematical model that we use to predict where and when our customers would need our products. This new model allowed us to separate our products into those that were in high demand in each region, and those that were still ordered, but in less meaningful quantities. This prioritization led to a radical rethink of the way we organized our supply chains, and ended up saving HP $500 million between 2005 and 2008.[6] Our customers noticed that the products they really needed were delivered faster than the lower-priority items.

The nature of the modern, competitive business market can be aggressive, even confrontational. Frankly, I love it. It's a rush to know that your competitors are out there, developing their own innovations and products, and that it will take all your wits and nerve to beat them to the punch. That's what makes it exciting. Of course, it also raises the stakes. It's critical that you constantly hone the skills you need to protect what you already have without stifling the creativity and innovation required to keep growing and developing both your company and your products.

THE HOW *KILLER QUESTIONS*

Before we dive deeper into the value chain, these first two *How* questions will challenge you to look broadly and think about how and where you look for ideas relating to your industry. Don't get caught in the trap of just looking at companies that are doing the same things you are. Look at industries completely outside of your sphere of experience. See if there are lessons that can be applied to you and your own work.

What industries are analogous to ours, and what can we learn from them?

No matter what business we are in, we are all fighting essentially the same fight—designing a service or product that a customer will prefer over that of our competitor. To do this, we need to constantly be aware of how our business environment is evolving, how our customers are changing, and what we need to modify in order to keep our product relevant and desirable. If you're in the business of making widgets, don't just look to other widget makers to get a sense of how you are faring in the global business space. Look at other businesses that have similar key elements in common with yours. I find the airline industry endlessly fascinating. It, like the tech industry, has gradually found ways to make its core products less expensive and more accessible to the general public. However, in return, *their* customers have had to accept a vast reduction in services and expectations. It's an interesting seesaw between what the customer truly wants and what they are willing to give up in order to get it. In the center are the core essentials: a safe, convenient flight at a low fare. Everything else falls away in relevance as long as the core criteria are met. What are the fundamentals that have to be in place in order to maintain an ongoing and happy relationship between you and your customer?

Suppose you were the head of operations at a megachurch. Perhaps Chicago's Willow Creek, or Joel Osteen's church in Houston. Osteen's church seats almost 16,000 people, and runs four worship services plus various meeting groups every Sunday, which means that there are up to 64,000 people—and the cars they are driving—coming in and out of the church parking lot in one day.[7] The sheer number of congregants means that the odds of getting into fender-benders, gridlock, and potentially dangerous traffic in the church's parking lot increases as one congregation departs and the next one arrives. So what do you do? Where do you go to learn the mechanics of moving that number of vehicles, and that number of human beings, in an efficient and safe manner?

If you're serious about solving this problem, you go to the Disney Academy at Disney World. Now, entertaining legions of small children with animatronic animals and teacup rides doesn't have much in common with preaching about God. But sixty years of crowd management has made Disney operations the undisputed champion of event control and coordination. By working with Disney, these churches could learn a few things about integrating their system of traffic flow and parking. Fender-benders would go down, customer satisfaction would go up, and everybody would be happy.

SPARKING POINTS

- What industries or businesses that are unrelated to yours are dealing with issues similar to yours? For example, issues of production, customer segments, or marketing.
- What are the lessons learned in terms of the push and pull between where those businesses are succeeding and where they are failing?
- What are some nonbusiness examples with similar issues to yours (such as foreign governments or a nongovernment agency like the Red Cross)?

What would happen if I realigned my industry relationships (i.e., partners, suppliers, etc.)?

Odds are that you and your competitors are actually competing in two distinct ways. The obvious battle is the one to win customers from each other. The less obvious, but equally important, one is the battle for the resources required to *produce* your product. In chapter 2, we touched on the concept of unexpected jolts, and how the disruptions they cause can be not only destructive but also an opportunity for a savvy company to make bold moves and leapfrog over their competition.

One way to prepare for jolts is to assess your relationship with key suppliers, and figure out if those relationships are strong enough to survive an unexpected event. Look at the suppliers who are critical to your business and ask yourself if you are a priority for them. If unexpected circumstances suddenly caused their output to be slashed, would you still get shipments or would you be waiting till the disruption was over? The tsunami that hit Japan in early 2011 was a disaster, both in terms of human pain and suffering and in the way it slammed down on the Japanese tech industry.[8]

Shin-Etsu, the world's top producer of the silicon wafers used to make semiconductors, had to suspend operations at their Shirakawa plant directly after the tsunami. They were only able to resume production there in July 2011. That's almost five months offline. Granted, they were still able to ship wafers from other factories, but the company's overall productivity was disrupted. Now, think of a key component supplier for your own business; if they went offline for five months, what would you do? Would you still be important to them, or would your orders be sidelined for months or even years till the supplier was back to 100 percent? In the aftermath of the tsunami, companies that relied on components from that region rushed to secure commitments from key partners in their Value Chain. Companies that had a purely buy-sell relationship found themselves struggling to secure key components. Those that had thought ahead and developed a deeper, more strategic relationship with the key partners in their ecosystem were able to get their components and continue to serve their customers.[9]

SPARKING POINTS

- Are there areas where you could establish a unique relationship with key partners and therefore block your competitors?
- What essential needs do you share with your competitors that are not obvious?
- How could you attract partners that would extend the value of your product (i.e., third-party accessories for smartphones, third-party car parts)?

THE VALUE CHAIN

A value chain refers to the pieces that need to be there for a business to be successful, such as product development, sales, marketing, manufacturing, and distribution. They include everything involved in coming up with the product and then turning it into something others will be willing to pay for. A well-functioning value chain is essential to all businesses, but I frequently find that smaller companies, such as some mom-and-pop stores, haven't given their value chain much—or any—thought. If you don't fully understand the individual components of your organization's value chain, use this chapter as an excuse to clarify which elements of your chain are working, and which aren't.

By constantly asking the *How* questions, you can challenge yourself to make innovations in your value chain and avoid complacency. Doing this will teach you to recognize and challenge your blind spots, as well as to see the dangers of "*You don't know what you don't know.*"

Remember, your competitors don't focus on *How* when they think of innovation. The *What* and the *Who* are the more natural areas to start. By even looking at the *How,* you are already a step ahead of your competitors.

The *How* Killer Questions are organized around a value chain, which I define as:

Research and Development
Manufacturing and Supply
Marketing and Sales
Shipping and Distribution
Customer Experience

Keep in mind that not all businesses use the same structure for their value chain. Your value chain may be different, depending on the products your business offers and the way it is structured. If certain elements of the value chain I discuss here don't apply to your business, that's OK. I'd still recommend looking at the relevant questions and seeing if there are other aspects of your organization they might apply to.

The point is that the value chain contains crucial information that is important for your business but that most people *don't* consider when they think about innovation.

Research and Development

You may not find a million-dollar breakthrough, and perhaps you are already taking full advantage of every possible by-product of your business. More likely, however, somewhere in there, there is an edge, an idea whose worth hasn't yet been realized but will either revolutionize your company or that of your competitors.

The point of these questions is to keep your eyes open to all possibilities when you are sourcing new ideas for your business. Where do your ideas come from? Are you outsourcing idea generation to a firm like IDEO, or do you rely on ideas from your internal teams? Do you believe that product ideas *always* come from your R&D department? Be careful that you haven't fallen into a pattern, developed a false sense of confidence, or begun to think that you've got yourself covered because all your idea sourcing comes from one source.

For example, recently I was eating lunch in the HP cafeteria. As I ate, one of the guys who worked in the kitchen came out and pitched me an idea. Now, all I wanted to do was eat lunch, but one of the results of being approachable is that people approach me no matter where they are on the totem pole at HP. The kitchen worker told me his daughter was struggling to do her homework because her hands were too small to use the standard-sized keyboard. He thought we should consider manufacturing a kid-sized keyboard for our PCs. I hear a lot of ideas that won't work, but sometimes I hear one that will. This one sounded interesting, and I would never have come across it if I hadn't opened myself to ideas from all sources.

What are the criteria to select research and development projects?

What are your criteria for deciding that an idea is worth pursuing? We all have our own set of selection criteria, the first of which is usually looking for profits. However, selecting a course of action based solely on ROI can be limiting. If you are doing something really innovative, how on Earth can you determine what the margins will be at an early stage of the product? The problem is, if you filter out new ideas based solely on whether they meet your financial projections, then you're going to miss some great—perhaps groundbreaking— concepts. As mentioned in chapter 5, when you get to the ranking phase of FIRE, ROI shouldn't be your first filter in deciding whether an idea is worth pursuing. When HP first got into printers, it was a tiny and not particularly interesting category. Now it's one of its highest profit-producing businesses. If HP had said, *Nah, not doing it; it's too small to be worth it*, it would have made a catastrophic mistake.

The printer division isn't the first example of where HP has made a tough call. Back in 1968, Bill Hewlett wanted to get HP into calculators.[10] He took the idea to the marketing team. They came back and said that there was no market for pocket calculators at that price. Bill said, "*I don't care, I want one of these things,*" and he made the decision to create it. And that one product was the catalyst for transforming HP from a test and measurement company into a computer company.[11]

I know from personal experience that projected ROI can be misleading. Be aware of your bias toward flashy and exciting numbers, and remember that figures on a page are easily malleable. Don't turn down an opportunity because you think the market is too small. When a guy comes in with a $200 million idea, and it piques my interest, I ask him, *How do you make this idea big enough to make me care? What do you need—more money, more resources? Are you being conservative in your estimates? How do you take this smaller idea and make it ten times better and ten times bigger?*

SPARKING POINTS

- What is the one key criterion that you must meet for a project to get approved?
- What would happen if you ignored this criterion in the evaluation process?
- What are the criteria used by others either inside or outside of your industry? Based on this, what would you change in your criteria?

Where do we perform product research and development? Where else could this be done?

What is your organization's philosophy about design and development? Do you keep everything in-house, or do you outsource as needed? There are two schools of thoughts on this. By keeping the design process in-house, a company can build a sense of continuity and cohesion that links the entire family of products together in a satisfying way. Or you can outsource as needed, hiring talent for specific products and moving on once that product is complete. Neither is right or wrong; the more important point is to have a rationale for whichever strategy you choose, and to extract the most value from it.

Look at a company like Herman Miller. Their Aeron chair is an iconic design for the technological age, but it wasn't designed internally. Instead, Herman Miller outsourced the design to leading designers who have their own firms. The famous husband-and-wife team Charles and Ray Eames designed the classic 1950s Eames chair the same way.[12] The point is that Herman Miller knows what their strengths are: manufacturing and distributing the final product. They also have a huge amount of practical expertise. For instance, they have experts in ergonomics, the less obvious details that are critical to the overall comfort and practicality of a product (e.g., the way a chair distributes the body heat generated by the user). They share this very specialized knowledge with designers, and then throw the company's expertise into selling the final piece of furniture. Herman Miller has a very different idea of where design, research, and development should take place. Herman Miller has adopted the philosophy that it's more important to ensure that the best and brightest are working on your product, and that this is a higher priority than making sure the work is done in-house.

Also, think back to the DreamScreen project I mentioned in chapter 6. When we began that project, we were very clear that we were going to make it specifically for India. So why would you design it in the United States? If you're going to design a product for a specific market, then you need to throw out the rules of how it's been done in the past and do the R&D closer to the customer. We sent a team to India, interviewed 2,600 customers, and drove the R&D from there.[13] Sometimes you have to put your resources in the right place to get the right results.

You need to be aware of the fact that your team will have gaps in their life experience, their beliefs, and their focus. This may not matter in 99 percent of the projects you assign them, but there will be times where these gaps are a problem. Consider the possibility that you need to look outside your walls to find the right brains for specific tasks. You aren't going to have 100 percent of the resources you need inside your organization; it's just too costly to keep these highly specialized people on the bench until you need them. If you are an employee in one of these specialized departments, you need to be aware of how this shift is going to change your value to your organization. If you believe there's a transition coming to the creative economy, then your future worth and career is dependent on your ability to come up with ideas for a number of companies rather than just one. As soon as you go dry, you are out of luck.

Another element of this Killer Question that you need to consider is the concept of open innovation, which has been a hot topic for the last few years. Open innovation is the approach where organizations go outside to secure a "funnel" of ideas. One example is companies who partner with state universities to leverage government-funded research, or companies who sponsor promising high school students in the hope that they will join their workforce after graduation. The

US government is using programs like TopCoder to create open-source idea channels. Companies like Procter & Gamble post tough engineering problems on dedicated websites and offer prizes for the first person to come up with a solution.

How does this affect you and your business? No matter what size your organization is, you have to recognize the importance of embracing the open-innovation concept as you source your ideas. One of the challenges with innovation today is that many people believe that high-impact innovation comes from large companies. However, the US Small Business Administration reports that while small firms are granted only 8 percent of all patents, they receive 24 percent of all patents issued in the top-100 emerging technologies.[14] Patents issued to small businesses are not broad, generic patents, but are focused on specific innovations that have the highest return. It's why you see so many examples of large companies acquiring these young innovative start-ups that are focused on a very specific area that is of interest to them.

This means that large companies are looking for sources of innovation outside of their four walls, and they realize that they need to be part of what others are doing, either by partnering with innovative start-ups, acquiring them, or investing in them. Procter & Gamble has a stated target that 50 percent of their innovations need to come from outside the company, which forces their people to seek out others who are doing interesting stuff, not just to rely on what's happening at home.[15]

Innovation used to be all about keeping things confidential and funding your own research and development. The future is different. This shift from the knowledge economy to the creative economy requires that organizations think differently about their funnel of innovations. The most valuable currency in the new economy is ideas, and ideas can come from anywhere. You don't need machinery or a lot of capital to have ideas. The creative economy relies on each individual's ability to come up with ideas that are interesting and compelling. These ideas can come from multiple sources, and you need to recognize that there are really, really smart people all over the world. In order to stay in the game, you have to be on the constant lookout for where that next great idea is going to come from. Because even if you aren't looking for it, I can guarantee that your competitors are.

SPARKING POINTS

- Are you doing your R&D 100 percent internally or externally, and do you really understand why you do it this way?
- How confident are you that you have the best possible research and development teams working on your projects?
- What would be the result if you radically changed your approach to R&D?

In what order do you do the R&D process? What would be the result if you flipped it?

In the traditional R&D process, the product is developed and then handed off to the design team to "wrap" it and make it look pretty. The drawback is that this approach is out of date; in the last ten years, consumers have become much more design-savvy. Consumers want functional, usable design that highlights ease of use, and is also emotive, adding a personal connection with the product or in some way broadcasting a statement about the user's more subtle, hard-to-define beliefs about themselves. We can all name a handful of companies that are melding form and function in a way that resonates with users and creates a deep-seated brand loyalty. Look at JetBlue. They are essentially a low-cost carrier, but their design does a masterful job of suggesting that they provide a full-service experience. Their terminal at JFK is a flashback to the old-world style of travel—more elegant and sophisticated than its customers would expect it to be, and more pleasant to spend time in compared with the terminals of most of its competitors, the so-called legacy carriers.

It's important to constantly ask why you develop your product elements in a particular order. This is especially true if your organization has been in business for a substantial length of time and yet you're still developing your products in an order that was devised to suit production methods from decades ago. Ford Motor Company worked with IDEO and the New York–based design firm Smart Design on the Ford Fusion.[16] This was a daring move for Ford, as the car industry has always believed in keeping new ideas proprietary. By bringing in outside firms, they risked their design being leaked prematurely. However, they recognized both that they needed to do something bold with the design to reflect the radically new nature of the car and that they didn't know where to start.

Ford wanted a design that reflected the fact that the hybrid car was something "new." Part of this process was realizing that their potential customer base was made up of people with wildly divergent needs and wants. There were the hard-core "hypermilers," who kept spreadsheets detailing the performance they got out of every gallon of gas. There were customers who were concerned about the environment but didn't think much about it beyond making the decision to go hybrid. And there were people who simply were looking to lower the amount they spent on gas but weren't emotionally invested in the environmental aspect of the vehicle. All of these groups wanted different levels of information and feedback from the dashboard array. The hypermilers wanted to "keep score" of their gas mileage and monitor how the car was performing at different points during their driving experience. The less environmentally focused customers wanted a simpler, less distracting display. In an initial survey of potential customers for the new car, the thing they agreed on was that there needed to be an easy-to-find clock display somewhere on the dash. So, rather than developing the dashboard last to meet the specs of the car (as it is typically done), the design team reversed the process and started working on the dash long before they even had the car itself designed. They started off interviewing hundreds of potential customers but quickly realized that no one design was going to make everybody happy. After multiple rounds of testing, they developed a dash that allowed the driver to pick one of four settings that determined what appeared on the display. Once this concept was finalized, it was sent to the engineers to incorporate into the overall specs of the vehicle. By reversing the order in which their process was normally done (here's the car, now figure out how the dashboard works within it), the combined team of Ford, IDEO, and Smart Design were able to come up with a unique experience that reflected the environmental philosophy of the car and gave users a customizable experience that was much more likely to please the individuals who purchased the vehicle.

SPARKING POINTS

- In what order do you develop an idea and its components? What would happen if you changed that?
- How did you make the determination about your customers' priorities in regard to how you ordered the phases of R&D?
- When do you involve design in the R&D? What would be the impact if you changed it?

Manufacturing and Supply

What are we throwing away because we assume it has no value?

My wife is famous for being a little frugal. She once routed me and our son, Logan, from Las Vegas to Phoenix to Los Angeles and finally to San Jose because she could save twenty bucks each over the nonstop fare. Kind of nuts, right? But if I'm honest, I have the same mindset in one respect: I am determined to squeeze everything I can out of any idea or opportunity that is available to me. I am diligent about looking at information and ideas that supposedly have "no value" and wondering, "Hey, maybe they do."

What I mean by this is simple. Just because you or your business has always operated under the assumption that something—be it data, ideas, or scraps from the manufacturing process—is essentially worthless, it doesn't mean that that assumption was ever, or still is, true. I constantly review the stuff that gets thrown away and ask myself, "Is there value here?"

One of my big breaks was becoming one of the early executives at Teligent, in 1997. Teligent provided phone service to businesses across the United States and in twelve other countries. The core products were voice and data services to businesses. There wasn't much to differentiate us from our competitors. Basically, we were all competing on the same fundamental premise: providing a good, reliable service at a cheaper price. Here's the problem with that: If there are no significant differences between you and your competitors, you are essentially in a stalemate, until one of you finds a way to differentiate yourself from the pack. So, even as our company continued to hum along nicely, I started asking the questions about who we were, what we were doing, and how we were doing it.

I started doing some internal investigating about the information we were gathering from our customers. After a little persistence, I got hold of the complete call-detail records for our network. In the telecom industry, the network throws away any record that isn't relevant to billing. The result was that 70 percent of the information in call-detail records was thrown away. A customer rang a business, the line was free, the call was answered, and a charge was added to the bill. Great, that's how we make money. But looking through the full call-detail records, I noticed something interesting: The logs showed not only the calls that succeeded, but also the calls that *failed*. For each business, there were pages and pages of incoming calls that weren't completed, usually because the line was busy, or the calls were coming before or after business hours.

This was information that was *thrown away*. We didn't bill for failed calls, so there was no need to document them or supply the information to the customer. But think about it—surely knowing that a potential customer tried and failed to make contact with you is invaluable information. Furthermore, isn't it the kind of information you would gladly pay for?

As soon as I saw the connection between this "worthless" information and our customers' needs, I got up, walked over to our CEO Alex Mandl's office, and pitched him a completely new kind of service that we eventually launched as e•magine. e•magine was a game-changing concept that allowed us to take a leadership role in the market. For a monthly fee, we offered our customers detailed breakdowns of all the incoming calls that failed to get through, as well as additional services like instantaneous e-mail notifications of each missed call. We supplied the names and addresses of every incoming call, so a business owner could then send out a coupon to every caller the next day. Sound simple? Think about the small- or medium-sized business owner whose margins depend on making every single sale. If that new customer doesn't get through to you, they are simply going to ring the next number in the phone book. They have no loyalty to you, and you've lost a sale and a potential long-term customer. *But* if you get instant notification of that call, and can ring right back, you've got a fighting chance. You're still in the game.

Our customers loved e•magine. By giving them the edge in their own business, we cemented their loyalty to ours. By taking something that we had historically *thought* had no value and creating something our customers valued out of it, we turned it into a game-changer.

Look more closely at your operations and stop worrying about the assets or attributes that you think you *don't have*. Instead, try turning inward and focusing on the question *What attributes do I not realize I have?* Our competitors had the exact same logs and information as we did; yet they didn't recognize their value. We saw that this information had worth, and we used it to clobber them.

Think it's a dumb idea? Zoos used to pay a small fortune to have manure hauled away. Then someone had the bright idea to package the manure and market it to gardeners. Now gardeners buy gallons of elephant manure for up to twenty bucks a pop and do the hauling for free.

SPARKING POINTS

- What information do you collect that never gets used?
- Are there by-products of your business that you are paying contractors to haul away? How could you flip it around and find a way to get them to pay you for this by-product?

What input, if reduced, would allow me to cut the price by 25 percent?

There is a reason that the percentage in this question is as high as it is. Sure, it would sound less scary and more reasonable if I asked you how you could cut your price by 5 percent, or maybe 8 percent, but that would be missing the point. If you want potentially game-changing moves to get ahead of your competition, you need to make big savings and do something bold to get to that leader-of-the-pack position. The best place to find these kinds of savings is in your biggest input cost. Don't settle for parity; look for those things that are a necessary evil in your business and see if you can turn them into a competitive advantage instead. If you and your competitor have the same basic cost structure and you can slash yours by a major innovation, well, you get the picture.

You need to continually look at ways to drastically lower the price of your product, because if you don't, it's possible that your competitors will. If you've ever driven in India, you've probably had some alarming near-death encounters with the brightly painted Tata trucks that fill the country's highways. They are huge, and rather than using their braking systems they rely on their horns to get other cars out of their way. About eight years ago, Tata decided to enter the passenger-vehicle market, despite the logistical difficulties of making the leap from manufacturing trucks to lightweight single-family cars. The car they came up with, the Nano, uses a two-cylinder engine and much less sheet metal than a comparable vehicle. Its trunk can hold one small bag, and it lacks a passenger-side mirror.[17] In other words, anything that is not strictly necessary to fulfill the mission of getting a family from point A to point B has been cut.

They are currently selling a car priced at under $2,000 in the Indian market. The cars have some issues. They are small, slow, and seem prone to catching on fire at inopportune times. Still, Tata is coming to the US market, and despite some production setbacks in India, it clearly has ambitions to succeed here.[18] If they do, it will radically change the nature of the domestic car industry. Would you buy your kid a $13,000 starter car if a similar model were $5,000 cheaper? US car companies have an opinion about who their customer is and what their customer expects to get from (and to pay for) a car. And it could prove very dangerous for Detroit if Tata figures out how to connect with US drivers and start making meaningful sales. If US car companies are going to defend themselves against hungry and aggressive competitors like Tata and their Chinese equivalents, they need to be careful. These companies have no assumptions or expectations about how they might sell their cars in the United States. Nor do they have a history of hitting certain price points or any expectations that a car is only worth selling if it brings in a certain amount of profit. They have different philosophies of what a car needs to be in order to satisfy their customer. What if the US customer starts to agree with them? Look at the sudden explosion of unrest in the Middle East and the resulting upswing in oil prices. Suppose things get worse, not better? A company that knows how to use minimal materials and resources to build ultra-cheap, ultra–fuel efficient cars, and isn't afraid to charge rock-bottom prices for them, is going to have a huge advantage in the US marketplace.

It will take a cognitive sidestep for Detroit to respond to ultra-cheap imports from the third world. Hopefully, you are willing to take that kind of sidestep, both to develop your product and ensure you aren't leaving any gaps for a competitor to sneak something game-changing into the marketplace.

SPARKING POINTS

- Which 20 percent of your components drive 80 percent of your costs (the 80/20 Rule)? Are they the same for your competitors?

- Are there innovation targets that could radically change that? Could you get a distinct advantage in your cost model by using an alternative?
- Are you offering things that you can eliminate because the customers don't attribute any value to them?

Marketing and Sales

What is the process used by my customer to discover my product?

Do you have a digital twin? The concept first formed on consumer sites like Yelp, but it's becoming a catchphrase in marketing and sales. The idea is that dedicated users of sites like Yelp eventually notice that there are other users whose tastes, interests, and "favorites" match their own. These digital twins do not "know" each other in the traditional way. They most likely never communicate directly with each other, but a link forms as one person realizes that the other seems to like or dislike the same brands that he or she does. Both twins' tastes align across a number of sites. People start to trust these twins to the point where they bypass the process of reading multiple reviews, and simply check to see what their twin thinks. Eventually, people start to value their digital twin's opinions over their own.

Recently, I was looking for a barber, since my previous one made the inconvenient decision to retire. I went on Yelp and found a local husband-and-wife shop that had more than a hundred five-star reviews. I showed up one Saturday for a cut. Sure enough, the line was out the door and the service was great. Now, I've never met any of these reviewers, but my instinct was to trust the collective voice of the group. This is a huge change from the old days when I would have gone into work and asked my buddies in the office for a recommendation.

The power of the anonymous point of view has been amplified. And it is incredibly hard to control. Customers used to be much more influenced by sales guys in making the big purchases, but now an individual can walk into a store already sold on what brand and item they want—even if it's an item they have no real experience with or knowledge about. So what's the end result? There's been a huge swing in influence. The individual voices of happy or dissatisfied customers has been amplified—way beyond the power of an individual voice in the pre-Internet era. Brands have lost some control, and advertising or sales reps are losing their ability to influence the sale. This is a huge shift from how people used to be swayed in making their buying decisions.

Customers are relying on sites like Yelp, digital twins, and other forum sites because they want to *reduce bias* in their purchasing decisions. We are all savvy to the way advertising or paid product placement can influence us to buy things that might not be right for us. We weight our purchasing decisions more heavily toward these anonymous voices because we think that doing so will help us to make better decisions. We want our decisions to be less about who has the best advertising campaign and more about who has the best product.

Granted, most users are sophisticated enough to understand how these review sites "work." A small number of highly positive reviews are a less accurate reflection of the actual experience of buying from this store than a larger number of mixed reviews. Once you get north of fifty or a hundred reviews, the sheer volume of reviews makes it harder to game the system. Users know that they can throw out the extreme reviews. The very low and very high scores are most likely biased, and can cancel each other out. Once these extremes are gone, you are left with a more meaningful and less corruptible medium review.

The key element of using a digital twin to reach and influence your customers is to find that one person who is so central to a network that they sway the opinions of others. Or, perhaps more interestingly, explore how you can replicate the experience of a digital twin for your customer in a more controllable, less organic state. How can you give your user the feeling that your product is approved of and supported by someone whose taste is trusted by "the crowd"?

Digital twins are the next logical progression from using celebrities to promote products. These anonymous voices can become highly targetable and very localized microcelebrities who have a sense of authenticity that comes from the social media they use. So, how will you use them to your advantage?

SPARKING POINTS

- How are your customers influenced to buy your product?
- How will your customer discover and select your product in five years?
- How could you get your customer to buy your product if you stop paying commissions or buying advertising?

What sales approaches need to be developed to reach new customers?

Lately, I've been hearing a lot about the impending retirement surge caused by baby boomers finally leaving the workplace and how it will affect changes in the tech industry. The combined worth of this market segment is roughly in the $2 trillion bracket. That's a lot of disposable income—and a lot of freed-up time for them to engage with new products, new hobbies, and new life goals. I mention the boomers because they represent a truth about customer bases: They are always in flux, and you need to constantly be thinking about how you can modify your sales approach to appeal to them. When you're looking for ways to reach out to new customers, keep in mind that you need to think of new ways to reach *existing* customers as well. An existing customer base still has the potential to change so radically that it can essentially become a *new* customer base as their passions and needs change over the years.

I've been interested to see how the health-care industry responds to the evolution of its existing customer groups, and the influx of new groups of aging patients dealing with the chronic diseases associated with age and poor lifestyle choices. A number of companies have become interested in using technology to support health care by reversing the idea of a patient traveling to see a specialist. These companies are in trials around the broad concept of "remote medicine," which allows for highly interactive virtual medical appointments. A nurse examines a patient while a specialist—perhaps in another city, state, or even country—observes and directs via video conference. The nurse and the equipment can be stationed either in a local doctor's office, or potentially in a mobile clinic. This is a huge boon for a massive section of the population—those people who live hundreds or thousands of miles away from specialists but require frequent appointments and checkups. Remote medicine companies have upended the traditional experience of how a patient and specialist meet and interact. By doing so, they have created a system that has the potential not only to vastly reduce the associated health-care costs but also to allow a whole new customer group to utilize their services.[19]

SPARKING POINTS

- How are you currently reaching out to new customers?
- To what extent do your sales approaches determine who your customers are? Is this a good thing or a limiting thing?
- What would happen if you applied a sales approach that is radically different from the one you currently focus on?

Shipping and Distribution

What new distribution channels need to be created to reach customers?

Are you in a serious relationship or married? If so, how did you meet your spouse or partner? I work with a lot of young single people and most, if not all, of them have tried online dating. Some of them are young enough that the idea of *not* using online dating sites is incomprehensible. Since Match.com went live in 1995, online dating has become an acceptable way of meeting your partner, if you are lucky, or, if you are unlucky, going on a lot of first dates with people you hope never to see again.[20]

Now, if you look at successful relationships as a commodity, then the creators of Match.com were also the creators of a radical new distribution channel for a product. Yes, online dating is following in the footsteps of lonely-hearts newspaper classifieds. However, the instantaneous nature of online dating, combined with the bottomless pool of "potentials," has radically changed *How* people set about finding their partners. It has also dramatically changed their expectations of what qualities that partner should have, and what compromises—if any—they should be willing to make.

Early in 2011, Match.com, a paid site, purchased OKCupid.com, a free dating site.[21] OKCupid had been very vocal about how paid sites work against users' interests by artificially inflating membership numbers or counting both a couple's engagement and marriage toward final tallies of successful relationships. It will be interesting to see how the two sites coexist and merge their opposing distribution philosophies, and which proves to have the most success in the marketplace.

It will also be interesting to observe how the central promise of online dating, endless choice, changes how people go about selecting and committing to a partner. In other words, how the evolution of the distribution channel changes the entire concept of what the product in question is, and what role it plays in the customer's life.

SPARKING POINTS

- How much of your customer's "share of wallet," or total spend, is going to different distribution channels? How is that changing?
- How are these new distribution channels changing the capabilities and features of your product, as well as how your customer values your product?
- What new distribution channel not in existence today could create a unique competitive advantage for you?

Can I reduce by half or double my distribution cost?

The other day my daughter Rachel ordered some shoes from Zappos. She's used them a few times in the past, and the next morning she got an e-mail saying her shoes had been shipped overnight as a reward for being a good customer. Now, one of Zappos's gimmicks is that shipping is always free, but you can pay more to get your shoes sooner. Persuading customers to pay more for next-day shipping is a core part of many online retailers. It's the same kind of upsell you get when your waiter convinces you to order the Italian artisanal water, rather than tap. What most people don't know is that whether you opt for free shipping or expedited overnight delivery, your book or shoes still ship via the same service, across the same route but at a lower priority.

FedEx and UPS have both taken interesting steps to maximize the speed with which they can ship their customers' deliveries. FedEx has businesses that are actually located within its SuperHub in Memphis to minimize the turnaround and delivery time.[22] UPS has customers who stock their spare parts at the UPS hubs. For instance, car manufacturers who need to have parts available almost instantly to dealerships and mechanics, but don't want to distribute them before they are needed, can store them with UPS and have the company pull and ship them as required. In some cases the part can get from one area of the country to another on the same day. These manufacturers see some savings by not stocking and tying up inventory. More important, they can offer a huge improvement in customer service by the quick turnaround of parts. The large express shipping companies have built an amazing business by creating a perception that overnight shipping is "the new normal." Interestingly, this new normal is often in excess of what the customer needs. I can't be the only person who occasionally fails to open an overnighted package the day it arrives. Look at your own organization. What experience are you trying to give your customer through your distribution? Do their needs and yours align? If not, could they?

SPARKING POINTS

- What value does your customer apply to speed of delivery? How does this value change depending on the buying season?

- Is there a way to use distribution to create customer loyalty?
- Is there a way to combine distribution costs with partners or suppliers to reduce overall costs?

Customer Experience

Customer experience can mean different things to different people, but for simplicity's sake, I think of it as the experience across the life-span of your product, from discovery and purchase to dealing with support issues toward the end of the product's life. All of these elements have to satisfy customers' needs and wants while creating a relationship that keeps them purchasing, using, and liking your product.

What do people not like about the buying experience for my product?

When I first started writing this question I played around with the phrasing. I considered asking "How can I make the experience of buying my product more pleasurable?" When I really thought about it, though, I realized that this is a classic mistake. The customers you really want to talk to are the people who had a choice between your product and another product, but chose your competitor's product instead of yours. Now, how are you going to get in touch with those people? I've mentioned before how I liked to observe potential customers purchasing or rejecting HP's products in big-box stores. If they rejected them, I would strike up a conversation and find out why. This is the most effective way I've found to establish contact with "almost" customers. After all, they didn't buy your product, so they didn't fill in any kind of warranty card or give you their contact information in some other way. Yet their feedback is invaluable. It's the same concept as the complaint card. Complaint cards, whether analog or digital, seem like a good way to gather and review negative feedback. The problem is that you only get responses from people who are really, really angry about their experience with your company. You don't hear from the much bigger group of people who rejected what you do for less dramatic reasons. You are missing the customer who experienced just enough friction with your product that they didn't want to purchase it, but who didn't care enough to actually contact you about it. These are the bulk of missed sales opportunities.

If you can find a way to communicate with these "almost customers," then you start to understand what they don't like about what you do and try to remove the issues that are actively working against their (and your) interests. It may be that you can't make them actively like your product, but if you can take away the aggravating or frustrating elements of purchasing it, that's just as good.

Look at your own experiences with purchasing products. What are your reasons that some experiences are positive while others are negative? I'm not afraid to negotiate or push for a better deal, but I still dread having to buy cars and houses. There are two reasons for this: One is simply that on some level you know you're getting taken. You walk into a dealership knowing that they are always at least one move ahead of you. My second issue is that I know what I want. The only house I've ever owned that truly made me happy was one I designed and built on my own. All the other houses I've owned have fallen short, and I've been happy to move on from them. These are pretty universal feelings. Nobody likes feeling like a rube, and everybody knows what they need from a product in order to be satisfied with it. Two car companies have led the way in providing these experiences to their customers: Saturn and MINI Cooper.

Think about your experiences with buying cars. Going to a traditional dealership is often tainted by the sense that the slick sales approach means you're being duped. Buying a used vehicle is a crapshoot that lacks any certainty or guarantee about the quality of the product. Yet this stressful and unpleasant experience is also the customer's expectation of what the experience will be like, and in a sense you aren't necessarily *disappointing* your customer by providing a difficult, stressful situation. By identifying these hassles and doing the opposite, two car companies, Saturn, and more recently MINI Cooper, have managed to create buying experiences that upend their customers' expectations.

Saturn thought long and hard about *How* they developed and sold cars to their customers, and how they kept that relationship alive over the years after making a sale. They asked their potential customers, *What is it you don't like about the experience of buying my product?* The number-one answer was *haggling with the dealer.* Nobody wants to look like the idiot who paid too much for a new car, or who got taken because they didn't understand the terminology of the contract. Saturn took the fear out of making a complicated purchase. Customers actually enjoyed the process of dealing with the noncommissioned salespeople. They found that the price on the sticker was the price they paid.[23] This simple switch in how Saturn sold their cars and built a fantastic relationship with their customers also led to a strained one with their parent company, GM. Ultimately GM hesitated to grant Saturn the full autonomy it needed to thrive (for instance, it refused to allow Saturn to develop their own, unique product line, and insisted that Saturn build their models on existing GM platforms). Instead, GM tried to keep Saturn integrated with the larger company. If Saturn had had more autonomy from GM, it might have survived. In 2010, Saturn stopped production.[24]

MINI Cooper is a great example of a company that offered a fantastic product for a targeted customer but also spent a lot of time and energy in looking at how they were making connections with their customer, and getting their product to market. First and foremost, the MINI is a great car. It's fun and quirky and says something about the driver. But at the end of the day, it's still just a car, right? MINI understood that if they wanted to make a dramatic and long-lasting connection with their potential customers, they had to give more value to them. They came up with a variety of ways to bring their customers into the process of building, customizing, and transporting the car. Customers could order the car online and spend hours sifting through the customizable features, "building" their vehicle. Once you'd made the decision to actually buy it, you could track the car online and know instantly when it was actually delivered to the dealership. The car was delivered with an autographed picture of the people who'd built it. Most MINI owners I know identify with their cars so much that they have given them names, and this kind of loyalty is invaluable. These people aren't simply car owners, they are brand ambassadors, and that's the best advertising you can ask for.

SPARKING POINTS

- How can you find your noncustomers to help understand why they didn't buy your product?
- How are you succeeding or failing in giving a differentiated buying experience to your customer? What could you do differently?
- Who is giving their customers a great buying experience outside of your industry whose practices you could adopt?

How can I cut the transaction time a customer experiences with my product?

I mentioned in chapter 7 how my wife loves to look for travel bargains. Her main goal is to save money, and she considers spending several hours comparison shopping a fair tradeoff for savings. I'm kind of the opposite; in the very rare instances when I have to make my own travel plans, all I want is to find the least-annoying flight as quickly as possible. Recently, I've started checking Hipmunk, a travel aggregator that uses an extremely simple layout to find you flights ordered from least annoying to progressively more annoying (long layovers, overbooked flights, etc.). Hipmunk has been smart to realize how the so-called paradox of choice can turn a relatively simple shopping expedition into a drawn-out and time-sucking endeavor. By simplifying the visual clutter, minimizing the input a customer has to enter, and steering you toward the least-aggravating choices, sites like Hipmunk limit the transaction time customers spend on their purchases. In other words, by seeming to offer you less, they actually offer time-sensitive customers more.

Of course, there are risks to this. I happened to stop at my local

IKEA the first weekend they transitioned over to self-checkout. They had made the somewhat questionable decision to replace all of their traditional checkout lanes simultaneously. The backlog of frustrated, angry, and eventually furious customers eventually led to hundreds of shoppers—including me—abandoning their carts and walking out. If you're an established business and you're going to make a radical change to the transaction experience, do it gradually or risk alienating your existing customers and destroying what goodwill you've already built up.

SPARKING POINTS

- Are you currently offering your customers options they would willingly trade for a faster transaction time?
- What is the equivalent of the 80/20 Rule when it comes to the time a customer spends with your organization?
- What parts of the transaction can be eliminated or combined to achieve a competitive advantage?

THE FUTURE OF HOW

Your customers will change the way they use your products in ways you don't currently anticipate. Do you remember when you got your first cell phone? I was living in Chicago when the city was selected for the first FCC trial of a cell-phone network in 1984, and I jumped at the chance to try this new technology. I had the stereotypical Gordon Gekko brick. For all its cost and glamour, I could do one thing with it: make a very expensive phone call. Who could have predicted that cell phones would morph into catchalls for our entire existence? With the improvements in technology, you can now run every facet of your life off a Windows, iPhone, or Android device. I was in the industry, and even I couldn't imagine a day when cell phones would move beyond sales-people and high-powered executives to become ubiquitous with the general public. Remember, being prepared for the future doesn't mean being a psychic or a mind reader. I am very aware that I don't *know* what's going to happen. What I do know is that I need to be flexible and responsive, and that the people and operations I oversee need to have the fluidity and fast reflexes to respond along with me. I don't know what the next Twitter will be; the only thing I do know is that there will be a "next Twitter." Five years from now, there will be a radically new and different way of communicating with your customer. It may seem nuts at first (140 characters, really?!), but it will quickly become essential. If your kid or assistant comes to you with an idea that sounds crazy, or an idea that you tried and failed with ten years ago, pay attention to him.

What will your industry's value chain look like in five years?

I'm a fan of the magazine industry—in fact, I've always been a magazine hoarder. I have a copy of the every issue of *BYTE* magazine. I love *Wired*, in all of its international editions, so my home office is stacked with copies of *Wired* up to the windowsills. I was heartbroken when the print edition of the design magazine *I.D.* was discontinued. Yet the writing seems to be on the wall for magazines in general—not so much that they will cease to exist, but that they will cease to exist as we currently know them. Just as is happening with books, in a few years our understanding of what a magazine is will have fundamentally changed. It will be interesting to see what a magazine subscription will look like in five years, or if readers will be able to pick and choose the elements of the magazine they want to read and buy them piecemeal. Perhaps journalists will be paid based on the number of readers who opt to buy an individual piece of their writing. Maybe magazines will go "smart" and tailor content for the reader directly. Either way, it seems inevitable that magazines will strive to emulate the blogs and websites that are beginning to replace them, but I do regret that we will have lost these small, fixed snapshots of a particular moment in time and culture.

You can't know now what the best choice for your business is, but you must be prepared to take a chance and make a decision. I've never met Anna Wintour, editor of *Vogue,* but I would love to sit in on her publisher meetings. I'm guessing that the question *How will my customer discover and buy our magazine?* is coming up a lot these days.

SPARKING POINTS

- If you assume the same level of progress that your industry made in the previous five years, what will the value chain look like five years from now?
- What elements of the value chain will no longer be there in five years?
- What would be the effect of regulatory change on your industry? What regulatory changes can you anticipate now?

What will your company's value chain look like in five years?

So, how do you determine where you, as an individual or a business, will be in five years? You can't say where exactly you're going because you can't predict what's going to happen in the world. However, you can challenge yourself to change. In 2001, Apple's sales figures were in decline.[25] The company had yet to launch the iPhone, iPad, or iPod and was struggling to get their computer products into big-box stores that were primarily focused on PCs. Their small market share made them a low priority for most retail outlets, and the company was frustrated by their lack of control over their potential customers' experiences with Apple products. By opening their own chain of stores, Apple was able to control their entire value chain from start to finish.[26] The stores purposefully simplified and enhanced the customers' experience with Apple products, and today the physical stores alone pull in upwards of 9 billion dollars in annual revenue.[27]

Can you replicate this kind of experience in your own business?

Look at how companies in the health-care industry are adapting to the coming "gray wave." The gray wave refers to the way our population demographics are skewing older. Some of these people are childless, and they want to live independently longer. These people will, in the next ten to fifteen years, require nursing assistance or nursing homes to help them in their old age, and health-care providers are looking at ways they can refocus their value chain to provide the kind of experience that will satisfy the gray wavers.[28] The industry traditionally focuses on nursing homes and assisted living, but what the gray wavers want is to remain in their own house and keep the sense of independence that has defined their lives. Savvy health-care organizations are looking at a new kind of assisted living that offers gray wavers the chance to keep their independence but also offers them the safety and security they need in the event of falls or unexpected illness. When a gray waver signs up for this service, the company places sensors in their homes to ensure they are physically safe and haven't suffered any falls or unexpected problems. The monitoring system extends to such devices as wireless caps on medicine bottles that alert the nursing facility if patients haven't opened their medicine bottles to take their medication. If you don't trigger the cap, you'll get a call reminding you it's time to take your pills.

This is a fundamental shift in the value chain of assisted living. Traditionally, "assisted living" meant that the customers lived within the four walls of a facility that in many cases stripped them of their sense of independence and autonomy. This model worked for years, but the technology for an alternative didn't exist. Now that the technology is available, the value chain has to evolve. By doing so, nursing homes can continue to give a generation of people who prize their independence above anything else the product they desire.

As you look at ways your value chain might change or evolve over the next five years, consider what will happen if your existing customer group goes away or their needs and wants change. If you are aware of these shifts, then you can change how you respond to them and ensure your customers are getting the experience they want and are willing to pay for.

SPARKING POINTS

- If you assume the same level of progress that your company made in the previous five years, what will it look like five years from now?
- What new elements will you need to create in your value chain over the next five years?
- Is your competitor better positioned to change their value chain than you are? Why? What would you do differently?

WHY HOW *MATTERS*

The business world is getting tougher, and it's critical to take any chance that you can to get ahead. Always keep in mind that the *How* is constantly evolving. For instance, if social networking is helping you to reach your customer and spread the word about your product today, recognize that you'll probably be using a completely different approach in the next few years. Don't assume your customers will still care about Facebook or Twitter, or that social networking will still look and feel the same. Ask yourself how businesses and customers will interact through the next few generations of networking sites, or if the ads on these future sites will still function as traditional ads. If the majority of consumers are relying on customer-feedback websites—and trusting what they read there more than the ads they are exposed to—then how do you get your message out?

By constantly reevaluating *How* you do things and how your value chain works or doesn't work, you can stay ahead of your competitors. Remember that most organizations neglect to really do this. If something feels comfortable and familiar, question why you are still doing it that way. Always ask yourself what might happen if you radically changed how you do things. Don't kick yourself a few years down the line because your competitor radically changed how they do things while you're still relying on out-of-date ideas and beliefs about your value chain. Keep asking the *How* Killer Questions, look at all the different individual steps that go into making your final product, and ask yourself, "*What would happen if I did this the opposite way of how I'm doing it now?*"

CHAPTER 9

Working the Workshop

I n the preceding chapters I've given you my system for using the Killer Questions to generate the quality ideas that lead to great innovations. Now comes your challenge: getting this information out of the book and into your organization. In this chapter, I'll give you a few essential rules for running a successful innovation workshop, including how to select the best people, how to get the idea generation process started, and how to avoid the most common mistakes that stymie the flow of ideas.

In my experience, most brainstorming sessions fail because they lack an effective plan. Recently, I was sitting with a friend, David, as he told me about his attempts to brainstorm ideas for his company. He was frustrated because he'd put a lot of thought and time into organizing the brainstorming session but hadn't seen any substantial results. I asked him to walk me through the process he'd used.

The first thing David had done was to decide that he needed to do *something*. He and his coworkers agreed that they were at a pivotal moment in their industry. Sales were down while new media, competing products, and new methods of distribution were challenging their product and way of doing business. They felt that the core issue was their company's ability to evolve and thrive as their industry moved to meet these changes. David wrote a quick e-mail, outlining this problem in clear language: "How should we change in order to align with the sweeping changes we see in our industry?" David sent the e-mail company-wide, set a date a few days later, and got eleven smart, motivated people into the conference room for a half-day brainstorming session.

At the given hour, the group assembled. After a quick introduction, David went around the room, and the group members took turns sharing their ideas and opinions. A volunteer wrote down the ideas and typed them up. The group ended on a positive note, and the participants felt that they'd generated some useful ideas—maybe one of them would come to something. The next day another e-mail was sent out, itemizing the ideas and inviting feedback. For the next day or so, a few group e-mails flew back and forth, mostly limited to "I like that idea," or "That will never work." By day three, these had petered out. My friend spent a few days contemplating the list. Then his boss gave him an urgent deadline. He put the idea list on top of his inbox and vowed to get back to it as soon as he could. The next thing David knew, it was a month later, and nothing had happened. The momentum and excitement of the group had dissipated. He felt deflated that nothing had been accomplished and was aware that he had spent a considerable amount of the group's "enthusiasm equity" in something that didn't work out. Even worse, he realized that his coworkers now had associated brainstorming with futility. The group members had worked hard but saw nothing come of their efforts, and they were likely to roll their eyes if asked to do it again.

I'm going to guess that most people reading this have been in a similar situation, whether they were organizing the group or simply participating in it. Workshops are an invaluable and essential tool— when they work. The group I just described made several key mistakes, any one of which is enough to derail a workshop and severely limit its chances of coming up with a killer idea that will accomplish anything substantial. None of these mistakes are flaws of character, passion, or ability on the part of the participants. They are simply in-herent weaknesses in the way workshops have been done in the past. They are the status quo, and thus can be hard to change, so don't beat yourself up if you've made errors like this in the past.

THE SIX GOLDEN RULES OF KILLER INNOVATION WORKSHOPS

Rule #1: Set a focus.

The first critical error David and his group made was failing to focus their attempt to generate ideas. As we've defined in the FIRE method in chapter 5, focus is essential in order to give people a targeted, specific area of investigation. Pick one aspect of your industry or organization, and decide whether you want to look at What you're selling, Who you're selling to, or How your business is operating. Use the assumptions questions in chapter 2 to help you isolate areas where you might be missing opportunities to innovate.

This strategy serves two purposes. First, participants given a focused topic are compelled to go deeper than they would on a general one. Many people make the mistake of thinking that by giving a group free rein to think about any aspect of the business, they will actually create a greater number of ideas. It's not the case. Second, focus not only pro-duces better ideas, it also reduces anxiety. The workshop is not a "snipe hunt" for ideas, it is simply a safe and open forum for them.

I asked David to put forward one focused area of inquiry that would be useful to explore in detail. He thought for a minute and sug-gested that they should look at the changes that would affect their customers in the future. They could also look at how their business needed to evolve to take advantage of the changing ways their com-petitors distribute their products. He added, "I'm curious about whether our distribution methods are going to be able to move fast enough in the future." All of these potential areas of focus fall into different Who, What, or How categories, but all are equally relevant to David's business. At some point in the future, he should attack all of them, but for now it's simply enough to pick one and proceed.

Rule #2: Assign two Killer Questions as homework.

It's critical to ask your group a set of well-written questions that will force them to look beyond the obvious. Simply suggesting an area of focus and asking for ideas will get you nowhere. It's too vague and too open to interpretation and preexisting biases. Let's say that our group decided to focus on the issue of how their customers' needs might evolve over the next five years. There are at least four or five Killer Questions that could be applicable, but giving your group that many options will overcomplicate your session. (Remember, this isn't a one-time-only activity; if more questions come up, you can hold additional workshops to address them.) Choose the two Killer Questions that seem most relevant to your particular situation. In this situation I'd go with:

What industries are analogous to ours, and what can we learn from them?
What will future customers' buying criteria be?

Two weeks prior to the workshop, send out these Killer Questions to your participants. Explain that you are looking very specifically for observations and ideas based around these questions. Be clear that you are assigning them homework, and that this homework requires getting out in the field and observing.

Rule #3: Encourage investigation.

The participants in David's group are busy people. They work all day, and then go out to industry events in the evening. On weekends, they sit at home reviewing projects that they don't have time to get to during the workweek. Sound familiar? David's original e-mailed question was so broad that it allowed all of them to apply it to aspects of their business that they already had opinions and knowledge about. His team "knew" how their customers felt about their product, and didn't feel they needed to get out in the field and actually investigate whether their beliefs were still accurate. The ideas they generated reflected this.

Rule #4: Don't filter.

We all have assumptions, and yours will kick in the moment you pick the Killer Questions and start thinking about your homework. Be aware of the biases that are going to pop up in your head. When you hear yourself think something like, "I know how to answer this question," stop. The whole point of this exercise is to force yourself to go outside of the old rules, so be aware when you default back to your safe and comfortable assumptions.

Rule #5: Set a schedule for generating ideas—and stick to it.

Don't tell yourself that you'll do the idea generation when you have time, because odds are it won't get done. If you are working by yourself, set aside fifteen or thirty minutes a day to focus on ideation. Organizing a workshop for a group serves the same purpose. Don't allow the session to go on for hours and hours, because you'll lose energy. Keep the time limited, and stay on point. Discussing the two Killer Questions should take about two hours. There's a reason for managing and limiting the time: You don't want to have to end the brainstorming workshop the moment the group has generated and collected the ideas—that's just phase one.

Think of your typical brainstorming session. What happens three or four hours into the actual process of generating ideas? Odds are, the energy and momentum you had in the first couple of hours is flagging. If you allocate a reasonable amount of time to generate and go over the ideas, you'll keep people fresh and engaged for the second half of the process, ranking.

Rule #6: "Ranking" isn't a dirty word.

Don't create lists just for the sake of it, because then you lack the focus about which ideas to go after. Always rank them; doing so is critical to a successful workshop. The whole purpose of the innovation workshop process, particularly when you get through the ranking and you start the execution, is this: You want everybody in the room to say, "You know something? These are the absolute best ideas we came up with today."

So, end your group at a point where all the participants can walk out of the room knowing that they have collectively selected the best idea applicable to the Killer Questions you asked them. This is key; you need that sense of accomplishment, and you need people to feel that the process is ongoing. You need your group to be invested in the idea and to be enthusiastic champions of it as it gets pushed forward.

COORDINATING YOUR WORKSHOP

So what do you need to know as the leader of an ideation workshop? A workshop has multiple elements—participants, Killer Questions, and so on—but at the end of the day, the quality of the ideas directly relates to your ability to create a highly functional, highly effective group. In this section I'm going to walk you through the way I set up and oversee my workshops. First, I'll provide a general game plan that you can use for your own workshop, and then I'll dive a bit deeper to help explain each step in detail.

But before we jump into how you actually run an effective workshop, I want to point out that there are two different scenarios. For the most part, I work with big organizations. The workshops I run have multiple participants, and there are representatives from all the relevant divisions present. However, this system is equally valuable to a small business or an individual entrepreneur. Don't be discouraged if you are a one- or two-person operation. I'll give you ideas for how to maximize your workshop throughout this section. One suggestion I would make if you are on your own is to form your own "executive board." Find a great group of people who are either connected to your business in some way (your lawyer, your accountant, angel investors)—people whose business savvy and experience you respect—

or are simply wise friends whose opinions you seek out anyway. Get two to five people involved and passionate enough that they'll participate in your Innovation Workshop. It's perfectly possible to walk this road alone, but it's easier with a little help. Don't be afraid to ask for it.

Preparing for Your Workshop

Recruit Group Members

The ideas you generate in your workshop are only ever going to be as good as the people in the group. I am a big believer in making groups as heterogeneous as possible. I want people of different ages, races, education levels, economic statuses, and beliefs. Theoretically, I want twenty-three-year-old inner-city scholarship kids sitting next to corn-fed engineers three times their age, senior management next to designers and enthusiastic interns, and so on. Big ideas are born out of being surprised when your expertise is challenged with a new piece of information. This won't happen if you all "know" the same things. Get participants from as many areas of your organization as possible, and keep the doors open to all comers as much as is feasible. At the same time, you need to find people who will actively and eagerly participate. Some people have the right credentials but don't contribute to the group, so you as the leader need to understand the dynamics of each person. I track how effective people have been in previous workshops. If they are active, dynamic, and great contributors (building on others' ideas), they get invited back. If they are lumps on a log or overly critical of others' ideas, they don't.

Select Focus and Killer Questions

Some group organizers have an immediate area they know they need to focus in on. Their organization may be losing customers and need to find ways to either reengage with their existing demographic, or find ways to attract new customers. They may realize their product needs to evolve, or that their way of doing business is growing obsolete. However, if you don't know where to focus, you should either use the assumption questions to help you zoom in on one, or simply pick among the Who, What, or How categories.

Once you've homed in on your area of focus, turn to the lists of Killer Questions, and select one to three questions from the appropriate list. Remember, you're looking for questions that you can't currently answer, or even guess an answer to. If you look at a Killer Question and think, "I know the answer to that," then your group participants may well have the same reaction, and you won't get the level of new insight you need.

Don't be afraid to rewrite the questions. Over the years, I've found that the wording of the questions is critically important. Be specific about where the question is being aimed, especially if you are going after an area that is a touchy or difficult subject for your organization. Use language your teams will understand, but at the same time, watch out for words that are overly familiar and loaded with meaning. Words have unique connotations at different organizations, and if you don't understand the nuances of how those words are understood, you may cause people to assume you are asking a much narrower question than you really are. Bear in mind that the questions in this book use the word "product," but the questions can be used for "services," "solutions," etc. Use whatever word works for your organization. The word "product" is widely assumed to mean *hardware* at HP, and if I ask a Killer Question related to product, people will assume I'm talking very specifically about hardware. If I'm looking for a broader set of ideas, I will use the word "solution." Be careful of words that have evolved to mean something beyond their dictionary definition in your organization, or come weighted with baggage. Changing a familiar word to a less-expected one may be an easy way to give you a radically different response.

Give your group the area of focus and the Killer Questions two weeks before the date of the workshop. Make sure that your participants understand that they have homework, and that they are expected to show up to the workshop prepared. They need to get out and observe. One important note: it's essential to start the process in a very focused way; however, you should still have a plan for addressing ideas that don't fit into your chosen area of focus. For instance, a group member may make a fantastic observation about how you are manufacturing your product while investigating who the customer is. If that happens, don't ignore it. Add it to the list of ideas to be considered at a later date. There are no limits to where ideas can come from.

Do Your Homework

Once you have assigned your Killer Questions, briefed your group, and set the date for the innovation session, it's time for everyone involved to do observational homework. This is exactly what it sounds like. You need your team to get out of the office, into the real world, and make as many observations as possible related to the Killer Questions. Your team can make these field trips as individuals or pairs, but they should avoid big groups. Big groups allow people to hide and not participate, and a larger-sized group can be slower and lethargic compared to smaller groups.

The first thing to decide on is where your observational session will be most useful. For example, if you are focusing on your consumers, then you must head to where your consumers generally experience or purchase your product. Once there, you should talk to them. For some questions, you might want to talk to salespeople as well as your internal marketing and sales teams—the people making purchasing orders for distributors.

So where exactly do you go? You could start in the mall, or your offices or factories—anywhere you or your customers conduct business. Wherever it is, get out there and really engage them. Remember that the dynamic between an organization and its customer is as complex and nuanced as any other relationship. In order to sell to a person you need to understand the details of their life. Are they in groups or shopping alone? How do they appear? Are they ambling contentedly, or do they appear in a state of distress? Do they make purchasing decisions quickly or spend ten minutes wavering between shampoo brands? What is your gut feeling about the people you are observing? Does their physical appearance match the image you have in your head? What is their emotional state, their level of financial security? What can you tell about their priorities and beliefs? Is there anything here that surprises you?

When we were developing our tablet device, we went to coffee shops in New York City and recruited members of the laptop-and-latte world, asking them to allow us to conduct in-home observations. This was several years ago, in the pre-Kindle era, and we were still investigating what customers would actually do with a tablet. We knew it could work as a digital book, but limiting it to that use seemed constraining. A digital book was a good idea, but could we press further and come up with an even better idea? For a few weeks, our researchers shadowed the volunteers around their homes. We photographed their book and music collections and noted their magazine subscriptions and TV habits. We figured out what people were really doing with their free time versus what they told us they were doing with their free time. This investigation showed us that what our consumers needed was a device for media consumption across a wide range of media types (books, magazines, music, movies, TV, etc.). This kind of discovery is why you need to get out there in the field and observe your customer. Doing so can completely reshape your understanding of what they actually want from you and your product.

If your area of investigation is not focused on consumers—heavy manufacturing, for instance—you will need to tailor your homework to focus on this instead. Go to the plant and see how the factory operates. Talk to the guys on the line. Try ordering your product, try using it. Do whatever it takes to step outside of your experience and see your area of investigation from a fresh perspective.

Have your group note everything they see, learn, and think in relation to the Killer Questions. It could be totally left-field and seemingly unrelated to your bigger problem. Nonetheless, write it down. Take pictures or make videos or audio recordings. Collect evidence and create artifacts that you can share with the team in the workshop. This may feel uncomfortable, and if so, great! The idea here is for everyone involved to step outside of his or her experience and biases and see the customer or product from a different perspective.

If you're not working as part of a group, you can still use other people to *force* yourself to see things differently. In the past, I've taken along a friend of a different ethnicity, or strong-armed an out-of-town relative or my wife or children into coming on these kinds of field trips with me. When I do this, I observe them as *they* observe others. What are they seeing that I'm missing? The goal of all these exercises is to be a little uncomfortable, because this discomfort means you are shifting your perspective, and, quite literally, getting out of the comfort zone that is stagnating you and your work.

INNOVATION WORKSHOP TIME LINE

Two to three weeks prior
Recruit group members
Decide on your area of focus
Pick 1 to 3 Killer Questions and assign Killer Question homework
Set date for workshop two weeks after homework assigned

Day of
9:00–9:30 Brief overview
9:30–10:30 Share industry and company assumptions and rules
10:30–12:00 Discuss Killer Questions and share the results of the homework
12:00–1:00 Lunch
1:00–3:00 Get ideas up on board
    30 min Generate ideas
    40 min Posting/sharing
    50 min Grouping of ideas
3:00–4:00 Break
4:00–5:00 Rank ideas
5:00–5:30 Set follow-up session for group charged with making presentation of best idea(s)

RUNNING YOUR WORKSHOP

Sharing Homework Observations

Once everyone is settled into the meeting, it's time to share what you've discovered. I generally give a quick recap of our area of focus. I start off by asking the participants to share their own list of the assumptions and rules that define how the industry and organization operates. I find it's important to acknowledge them, and get them out on the table. By doing this, we can free up the workshop to focus on the ideas that we came to discuss. Then I'll ask the participants about their experience and to share what they observed. Don't go in a circle! I always ask who wants to talk first, and after that I'll look for facial expressions. Is there someone who's excited to share because their observations naturally build on the one we've just heard? Keep the sharing quick and focused; don't let them get lost in the weeds.

Each person talks about what they've observed. If they've collected images, videos, or physical artifacts, they should share them at this point. I prefer these artifacts to be physical instead of digital, so print them out and either pin them on the walls or pass them around. Don't fall back on PowerPoint. The more physical the artifacts, the more they will inspire the group as they think of ideas.

This is not about *generating* ideas yet; it is simply about sharing what they have observed. Remember that the answers to the questions are not themselves ideas. They are the input for what you are going to use to generate ideas.

Ideation

Once everyone has shared their input, we move to ideation. Start by assigning an idea quota. Now, you're not grading them on the quality of the ideas. At this point, we are simply looking for quantity.

Keep the energy high and don't let their minds wander and procrastinate before they are done. Keep the momentum going. Give the group twenty minutes to write down thirty ideas related to what was shared during the homework portion of the group.

The ideation stage is freeform. Have the team write down every idea that comes to them, without thinking about its value or practicality. I like using Post-it notes for this exercise so that the ideas are easy to share on a whiteboard or flip chart.

Don't be critical of ideas at this stage of the process. I'm a firm believer in the concept I call "stupid wins." It's natural not to want to look stupid by proposing a stupid idea, one that seems too dumb to work or to bother investigating. Yet brilliance is often deceptively simple, and by discarding ideas that seem too simple, you are putting yourself at a disadvantage. Why? Because your competitors most likely are throwing away the same "stupid" ideas. Their bias—like yours—is causing them to reject ideas and miss the same opportunities you are. So force yourself to look beyond the bias, and don't give up on the stupid ideas.

If you get stuck, try looking at the ideas you've already generated and see if any of them can be broken down into smaller components. Try the weird, random combination route; see if you can combine two ideas you've already come up with into a third one. Combine ideas with the person sitting next to you. If you have a good idea, write the opposite of it down. Does the opposite have value? For instance, in a recent education workshop, a participant suggested letting kids use their smartphones during class for educational purposes. If you were stuck, you might ask what would happen if you did the opposite and removed all electronic, computer, and communication devices from the classroom.

Sharing and Grouping

At the end of the ideation part of the workshop, have each team member take their Post-it notes and place them on a flip chart or other surface that everyone can see. Have them briefly talk through their ideas. Get through this process quickly. You don't need master's dissertations. Start to group the Post-its together if two or more people have a similar idea. Once everyone has their ideas posted, have the groups come up and finish "grouping" them into common categories, which they should then name. Pick the person who is clearly the most passionate about the idea to give it a descriptive name, and sum up the concept in a sentence. Get rid of any duplicate ideas at this point, and get to the core list of ideas.

Before we move into the ranking phase, it's also worth noting that when I run workshops over multiple days, I use the first day for sharing the observations. After the group has exhausted the ideas and grouped them, I'll break for the evening, have a relaxing dinner, and then pick it up the next morning. In the morning, everyone is refreshed, and ideas have had a chance to percolate. Whether you are running a workshop over one or multiple days, use breaks to allow your group to mentally "reset" between the different portions of the workshops.

Why is this reset important? Your subconscious will continue to work on solutions, even when you are not aware of it. In the mid-1800s, Elias Howe was struggling to invent a machine that could industrialize sewing, just as the new spinning and weaving machines had revolutionized the textile industry. He tried for years to create a machine that could stitch two layers of fabric together, but he could not find a solution. One night he fell into a deep sleep, and had an exceptionally vivid dream that spear-carrying savages were attacking him. When he looked at the spears, he noticed a hole in the tip of each spear. Eureka! The next morning he began work on a sewing machine with a needle that was threaded through the sharp tip, rather than its rounded end. His invention led to a complete shift in how clothing was manufactured, marketed, and purchased.

Howe's idea may seem like it came out of nowhere, but in reality, his subconscious had done the work of making the connections between everything he had been observing and thinking about. Like Howe, you sometimes need to just let the brain do what it wants to do and not stress about thinking about things all the time. If nothing is coming to you, step away from the process and let your mind relax before you try again.

The Ranking System

Before we start ranking, I want you to think about group dynamics for a second. Ideally, you will have somewhere between five and ten people participating in your ideation group. These people will be drawn from all divisions of your company, including, but not limited to, engineering, marketing, and executive. Some of them will be senior enough to be perceived as "the boss." All of them will have their own biases or filters for sorting out the ideas you present, and sorting them in terms of value.

As a result, what I find works best is passing out ballots and having your group members score ideas and hand in their votes privately. Don't ask for a show of hands or take people's votes verbally. You want your participants to feel empowered to have an opinion. Don't put them in a situation where they will feel foolish for disagreeing with either their peers or more senior members of the team.

The ranking system is simple. I use a five-question scoring system to sort out the best ideas. It's important that you make the commitment and follow through on taking the two or three best ideas and developing them into a proposal that will be presented to management.

Bear in mind that these questions are aimed at a business. If you are working the Killer Questions in other areas, you'll have to reword the ranking question to be applicable to your own criteria. If you do this, remember that the first three ranking questions are about the quality of the idea; the fourth and the fifth are about whether you can see a path to making the idea in question happen, and whether it's a meaningful endeavor for your organization.

One final note: Depending on the size of your workshop, you may end up with more ideas than might be convenient to individually rank. In this case, some companies have chosen to narrow their options with a pre-ranking system. If you'd like to do so as well, try using my "dot" method. Give everyone on the team a set of five "sticky" (Post-it) dots. Each person then places dots next to the ideas they believe are the ones that best meet the objective. If a person really likes an idea, they can put all of their dots on just that one idea, or they can spread them around. Using these dots, you can help narrow the field of ideas to be further ranked to a more manageable number.

THE FIVE QUESTIONS

Score your answers to each of the first three questions from 0 to 5. A 0 means that the idea being considered doesn't move the needle on this question (or, in other words, is a no-go for the time being), while a 5 is a resounding yes. You should ask these five questions for each of the ideas being considered. You're looking for both an initial yes/no response and an eventual score for the ideas that get the initial yes.

1) Does this idea improve the customer's experience and/or expectation?
   • Does this idea solve a problem?
   • Will it give your customer something they need and want?
   • Will it solve their problems in a unique and different way?

2) Does this idea fundamentally change how you're positioned competitively in the market?
   • Will this idea put you ahead of your competition?
   • Will it disrupt the market's idea about your organization?

3) Does this idea radically change the economic structure of the industry?
   • Will this idea disrupt the way value is created and monetized so that your organization benefits?

If you can't answer yes to one or more of these first three questions, then you're doing the same thing as everyone else, so why bother?

The last two questions are about whether the idea is a strategic fit for your organization. To have a killer idea, you must be able to answer yes to both of them. Score them the same way you did for the first three.

4) Do you have a contribution to make?
   - Do you have the experience and/or expertise to bring to the problem?

5) Will this idea generate sufficient margin?
   - Are the potential returns enough to justify the cost of pursuing the idea?

Just because you can do something, it doesn't mean you should. When I ask you if you can make a contribution, I'm asking if your organization brings some capability to the idea. HP has the R&D budget to explore a wide range of possible innovations, but they're not going to work on an idea that is too far outside of their industry or their core strengths. There needs to be some foundation to leverage from.

Finally, you want to figure out if this idea is lucrative enough to be worth pursuing. This is often a matter of gut instinct, since for a truly great idea, you won't have a precedent to determine its value. Think about it. If an idea is solid enough to get a yes on the first three questions, it should make money. As we said in chapter five, in most organizations, return on investment (ROI) is the first filter that an idea has to pass through if it's ever going to get funded. Setting ROI as your primary filter means that you will discard a ton of potentially great ideas, because there is no way to prove (to the satisfaction of the CFO and CEO) in advance exactly what the return will be. The determination of how much it will return will be the output of the stage-gate funding process. Don't get too hung up on *how much* but rather focus more on its potential.

Gather the totals for all the scores for each idea. One surprise that I've seen in hundreds of workshops is the clear grouping of the best ideas. There will be a grouping of a few ideas, then a gap in the score, and then the rest of the ideas.

Keep the top ideas to use now, but don't discard the rest. Instead, hold on to the master list of all ideas, and revisit it in a year or so, when the timing might be better for them. I don't specify how many ideas we should end with because it varies, depending on what the objective is for any given group. And always remember, just because an idea comes out with a top score, it doesn't mean it's the best idea to pitch. Once everyone is finished totaling their scores for each idea, you can gather the totals for all the scores and determine which ones are the best to explore further.

EXECUTING YOUR IDEAS

Which to Pitch?

The next stage is to consider how these ideas might be implemented by your organization. Look at the top ideas and say to yourself as the leader, "These are great ideas—how can we execute them?" The following questions will help you get to your answer:

Can we get our teams passionate about working on this idea?
Do we have the skills and abilities to do this?
Can I get senior management on board with this?

Senior executives are show-and-tell. In other words, you need to supply information to support the good ideas, but you also have to show them that people will care on an emotional level. So before you select the final two or three ideas that you are going to fully develop and present, ask yourself whether this idea is one that you're going to be able to create some sizzle with and get people excited about. Will you be able to create a vision that people are going to fall behind and want to be a part of?

These questions are about the potential difficulties of selling the idea internally. It's important to know that I don't ask all groups these questions. These questions can be very politically sensitive, and asking them to the wrong mix of people can provoke arguments and problems. You need to use your own judgment about whether asking these questions helps your group or will derail it.

You as the leader need to make the call as to which two or three ideas should be pitched to senior management. Before doing so, the ideas need to be turned into a proposal. Before the workshop ends, assign teams to each idea, and set deadlines for when the pitch needs to be ready. Give the team clear guidelines on the structure of the pitch.

Making Your Pitch

Keep the pitch simple, and build it around the Guy Kawasaki Rule of 10/20/30: 10 slides, 20 minutes, nothing smaller than 30-point font.[1] Remember that you are telling a story; you want a spokesperson who can bring the idea to life and get people excited. Practice pitching the idea before you take it to senior management, and fine-tune your pitch depending on the feedback. Include the Gated Funding Model, using the structure shown in chapter 5, to see what you can realistically convince your management to invest. You have to think through what the executive uses as decision criteria before you make the pitch.

Pausing an Idea

As an outcome of the workshop, you may find that one or more of the ideas may be great, but the timing isn't right. The customer isn't ready, the technology doesn't quite exist, or the organization isn't ready for the change. Pausing is a good option. Take those ideas that ranked high but for which the timing wasn't right, and place them on a list that you come back to on a regular basis. When the timing is better, it's time to pitch them to the organization. The key is to capture and track the ideas that come out of this and future workshops. This "idea management" step is one that is commonly overlooked. As I mentioned when discussing what happened to my friend David in his brainstorming session, typically a session is followed by a final e-mail sent around to the participants a few days later. The end result is usually that nothing happens, momentum is lost, and good ideas go to waste. You can't let this happen to you. If you organize and run your innovation workshop as I describe, you will have a ranked list of ideas that, if used, will create an innovation funnel for your organization.

||||||||||||

Here's one final thought before you go into your pitch meeting to sell your best idea. I was at HP for nine years, and over my tenure there, I launched twelve fundamentally new products. Each one of these launches was as much of a battle as the first; it *never* gets easier. In fact, I think that if it becomes easy, it means you aren't doing your job. Why? Because if it's easy, it means that you aren't giving people anything new enough to elicit that initial reaction of resistance and fear. This process is never easy; don't beat yourself up if you find that getting a great idea to the execution stage is exhausting, hard work. If it's a great idea, most people's gut reaction will be to push back against it. Persevere.

CHAPTER 10

Adopt and Adapt

I don't know what your needs are. I don't know what drove you to pick up this book, read it, and (hopefully) work through the exercises. It's possible you weren't completely sure of your needs at the beginning of this book either. However, you should now have a sense of how you can use the FIRE method and the Killer Questions to challenge the assumptions that may be holding you back. This chapter is about collating everything you've read and refining it into a program for your specific needs.

Every idea and technique in this book is customizable. There may be practical reasons why you can't assemble a group of people to brainstorm with. OK, then do the work solo. Maybe your value chain is so radically different from the one I've outlined that you need to create your own set of *How* Killer Questions to suit your needs. Great. Perhaps your ranking questions are completely different from mine. Only *you* understand the realities of your organization. Don't try to shoehorn your needs into this approach. Adopt what works, and adapt what doesn't. In this chapter, I'm going to run you through the various ways I adapted this very business-oriented program to assist in innovating at both a traditional company, Kroger, and in a radically different "industry," education. Again, your needs might still be different, but I hope the ideas presented here give you some idea of how you can customize *Beyond the Obvious* to create an approach that works for you and your organization.

KROGER: A CASE STUDY

One company I've enjoyed working collaboratively with is Kroger, a company with more than 300,000 employees. When I started working with them, they had been very successful in the grocery industry, and they had a way of doing things that had worked well for them for years. Yet they recognized that they needed to be open to change and look for ways to stay at the forefront of their industry—and they needed an institutionalized means of generating innovation.

As a result of their work over the last five years, the company has gone from not having an innovation team to having one of the most effective and passionate groups of innovators I've seen. One of the keys to this transformation was their team's realization that it would have been too jarring and radical to try to drop my approach, unchanged, into the corporate culture at Kroger. Instead, the innovation team there modified the ideas in this book to fit their needs.

The Kroger team was started by a (then) new-hire from FedEx, Brett Bonner. Brett was a long-time listener of my podcast, and when he arrived, his unorthodox methods instantly lit a fire with his new team. In his own unique way, Brett was shaking things up at a very traditional company and getting people to question their assumptions about how they fit into both the newly formed innovation team and the company as a whole. He got his team thinking about what was expected of them, and whether this expectation was accurate or limiting.

Early on, the team was introduced to my podcasts, and over the course of the last five years, the team morphed what they heard in the podcasts into something that worked for them. They don't focus on running formal workshops; in fact, the pace of innovation there is so fast that they are essentially in one constant, informal "workshop mode." The key catalyst for their innovation process is to get out there and observe their customers. All businesses need to be aware of their customers' changing needs and wants, but this is even more important when you are counting on your customers making small, constant purchases rather than one big-ticket purchase every few years.

One of the most interesting aspects of how Kroger uses the Killer Questions is that they've worked to implement a Killer Question mentality, in which employees understand that a Killer Question is about *learning/seeing/considering something you wouldn't have learned/ seen/considered otherwise*. They incorporate that mentality into their day-to-day observations, ideation, and innovation.

When Kroger does explicitly ask Killer Questions, they phrase them to reflect the realities of their business, which is that the company is very focused on profit and loss. They'll also use questions more generally to get the team to think creatively. For instance, they'll ask something like *What is the #1 ranked country in personal and business freedom?* This question works because our natural answer is "The United States, of course." In fact, the United States is further down the list, with Denmark taking the top spot for 2010. This kind of revelation shakes up people who may have a comfortable sense that, on some level, they are "at the top," either as individuals or members of a business or industry. As soon as you can throw a core assumption into question, you open up people's eyes to the fact that there are other assumptions that need to be shaken loose.

I believe in working quickly and creating and maintaining momentum throughout the innovation process, and the innovation team at Kroger has taken this idea to the extreme. They are responsible for generating ideas and innovations across the many different groups at Kroger. It's demanding work, and they need to turn ideas around, fast. To help facilitate this, they've staffed their teams with people from all over the various groups and departments that make up the greater company. These team members know where innovation needs to happen, and ask for help in particular areas. Once a request has been

placed—say, *I need a solution for the front-end system of the store*—
the team quickly generates a concept and a mock-up that's presented
to the relevant department. If it gets turned down, it is quickly shelved.
If it is approved, they start using their own version of the gated funding system and get a little bit more money, time, and focus to evolve it
further. The key here is that the innovation team is very busy, moves
fast, and doesn't spend a lot of time on tweaking ideas that didn't get
initial approval.

I think the Kroger team has been especially innovative when it
comes to execution. They realized early on that they couldn't expect
the established groups within the company at large to work with a
single version of the gates used in the FIRE execution phase. These
groups had been up and running for years, had ways of doing things,
and knew exactly what goals an idea would have to hit in order for
them to consider it worth pursuing. Each group had different priorities and a different way of doing things. It wasn't the groups' job to
change; it was the innovation team's job to meet the groups' needs
instead. I love how the Kroger innovation team was able to acknowledge that and tweak the system to work within the dynamics of their
company. They created a custom system of gated stages to match the
needs and wants of whichever Kroger group would eventually own the
innovation. This allowed those groups to quickly see the innovation
as "theirs," rather than as something that is being forced on them from
the outside. By adapting the innovation process to each department,
the team reduced the risk of corporate antibodies trying to derail the
ideas.

The innovation team did a similar thing to the ranking process,
customizing it to meet the needs of the various internal departments
they were innovating for, rather than trying to force those departments
to work to one unchanging set of ranking questions. Their ranking
system is relatively freeform, and by handing over the power and sense
of ownership, they've once again found they have a greater chance of
support from the core organization.

For example, as I've mentioned a few times now, I'm not a huge fan of putting too much emphasis on ROI in the innovation process. However, there are businesses and industries where trying to downplay ROI in the ranking process would create resistance and frustration between the team and the organization as a whole. The Kroger team has had to adapt the way they use ROI as a ranking tool to reflect the incredibly slim profit margins for their industry. Their reality is that they have to sell a lot of milk and bread to have just one dollar to invest in innovation. As a result, every innovation dollar has to justify its spend earlier in the process than I generally recommend. The team has accepted this central characteristic of their business, rather than trying to work against it.

By putting this process into motion, Kroger has used their innovation team to pull off one of the most significant innovations in grocery retailing: creating a scanning tunnel that really works. This innovation is particularly notable because developing technology that radically simplifies and speeds up the process of self-checkout has long been the elusive golden ring for grocers. With Kroger's system, when a customer is ready to check out, he can simply place all his items on the conveyer belt of the tunnel. Customers don't need to check and make sure the bar codes face a certain way, nor do they need to space out or organize items in any particular manner. The tunnel uses advanced technology to "see" each item and price it accurately, even with items that are sold by weight. As soon as the items are all on the belt, the customer can go around to the far end of the scanner and start to bag his purchases.

For Kroger, the core Killer Question concept was *How can we provide a high-end shopping experience at an acceptable price point for our customer?* The scanning tunnel allows Kroger to free up employees to work in the main areas of the store instead of at the registers, and provide the customer-first experience that sets them apart from competitors.

Kroger has done many things differently from the system I've outlined in the book, and they've seen incredibly successful results. They've adapted the ideas here to suit their corporate culture and the realities of their industry. The scanning tunnel will radically change the nature of their business, and I'm interested to see what else their innovation team comes up with in the future.

Your business or industry might require similar flexibility. Don't worry that you are compromising the overall effectiveness of your innovation process by tweaking the way you use the methods in this book. As long as you are actually getting out there, asking the Killer Questions, and generating ideas, you are on the right track. That's more important than trying to shoehorn a set methodology into your corporate culture.

THE DEPARTMENT OF EDUCATION: A CASE STUDY

About a year ago, I got a call inviting me to participate in a meeting with the Department of Education because they were actively looking at ways to innovate how kids are educated.

I agreed to participate in a meeting in San Francisco, and I was happy to have the opportunity to do so. My enthusiasm was partly due to my own desire to help rework the way kids are educated, and partly due to my curiosity about how the FIRE method and Killer Questions could be tweaked to work in a completely new arena: education. I have a lot of ideas about education; I believe that the way we educate our young people actually works against their best interests. Our attempts to give them a solid background in facts and figures, rather than teaching them how to *think*, hurts and hinders the people it's supposed to be helping. Instead of producing a generation of kids empowered to believe in their own creativity, we are producing the world's greatest test-takers.

A few weeks after the initial call, I attended a high-level meeting. But as the conference room filled with Ivy League deans and people with President Obama's cell on speed-dial, I wondered what the heck I was doing there. I have *very* strong opinions on education, but I had a sneaking suspicion that they wouldn't go down well if I shared them in this forum. The afternoon dragged on. Finally, the moderator asked me, "So Phil, what do *you* think?"

Now, I had plenty of thoughts to share. For instance, I could have mentioned that I have so little faith in our education system that my wife and I home-schooled all three of our kids. Instead, I looked around at the national union leaders, college presidents, heads of Association of Charter Schools, and a deputy secretary of education, then stood up and said, "I can't tell you how to fix the process, as I'm not an expert in education. I think of myself as a purchaser of your output. I hire scientists and engineers. But what you're producing, I don't want."

Silence.

A few months later, I was asked to join a conference call with the Department of Education to expand further on why I said what I said during the meeting. I shared my views on education and my thoughts on how they should go about generating ideas to innovate and improve. At the conclusion of the call, I was asked if I could come up with twelve Killer Questions that could be used in the classroom, schools, and school districts. Education is a hugely emotional topic, and the objective is to change the ongoing conversation between school administrators, students, parents, teachers, and taxpayers from criticism and attacks into a more productive dialogue that can generate ideas.

We've all experienced the process of education in one form or another, so why is it so resistant to innovation? Like all organizations, education is resistant to change. The old adage that "what was good enough for you when you were a kid is good enough for today" gives comfort and justification that everything is fine. Everything is not fine. The world our kids will need to compete in is radically different from the world ten years ago. However, our schools are training students to value depths of information and knowledge in single, specialized fields as opposed to creative and innovative sparks that have the potential to be applied in infinite ways.

The education establishment hasn't always been afraid of change, though. Ohio State University, like a lot of the early colleges in the Midwest, started as an agriculture school because that was the economy of the day. When family farms stopped being a viable and desirable business for young people, these colleges changed their focus to reflect that new reality. OSU, like many other former agricultural schools, is now focused on engineering.

So, what would you come up with if you were asked to think of twelve Killer Questions that would fundamentally reshape the way we view the education process in America? By the time this book comes out, I hope to have submitted a set of customized Killer Questions that may become part of the Department of Education's attempts to transform the way we educate our children.

Over the course of the next few pages, I will walk you through the process and the actual workshop I ran with the objective of coming up with a unique set of ideas that will be submitted for consideration. Unlike the Kroger case study, which demonstrated how a traditional company can adopt my Killer Questions, the Education Department is a good example of how an organization can adapt them, even to unexpected contexts.

Innovating in Education

The first thing I did after the phone call was post to my blog, Facebook, and Twitter. These posts generated the most feedback I've ever received on any topic. I got tons of suggestions, ranging from the provocative:

What if you tied teachers' retirements to their students' future earning ability?

To the amusing:

What if you adopted Jedi or Vulcan teaching practices?

I quickly realized that I needed a way to validate the education version of the Killer Questions before I submitted them to the Department of Education. To do this, I thought it would be helpful to hold a workshop as a dry run. Now, we covered how to run a workshop in chapter 9. However, this workshop was going to be different. I'd need a new set of Killer Questions tailored specifically to education, and a new way of ranking the ideas generated.

My first objective was to zoom in on an area of focus. I decided that this focus was *to create innovations in education to better prepare our students for the competitive workforce.* Then, I looked at it in terms of Who, What, and How. Who is the Who in this situation? What is the product? How does the value chain succeed and fail? Are you meeting your Who's needs? Keep in mind that Killer Questions are investigative questions that are constructed to force you to look at the widest range of possibilities, including ones that you've never considered before.

Next, I needed to identify the assumptions that people in education were working under. After all, "conventional wisdom" exists in all industries and organizations; education is not immune. Just as I discussed in chapter 9, it is important to reveal the rules and assumptions that hold back the ability to innovate and change. For the education workshop, I modified one of the core assumption questions in this way:

Before: What are the assumptions under which my industry operates?

After: What are the assumptions under which the US education system operates?

Some possible answers include:

- Standardized testing is the way to categorize students by their abilities.
- The education system is too big and unwieldy to allow for change.
- The optimal teaching time is five days a week, eight hours a day.
- Teaching should only be done by accredited teachers.

The answers that are generated from the assumption questions put everything on the table for discussion, even things that we see as hard-and-fast rules. For example, look at the last assumption I have listed up there, "Teaching should only be done by accredited teachers." On the surface, this makes sense; we need to know that teachers can teach. But if you think a little deeper, you realize that there are some major flaws in this. Surely a retired PhD, CEO, or other person with extensive life experience and knowledge has valuable information to share—perhaps even more valuable than a burned-out or disengaged teacher.

Look at the Khan Academy, which started in 2004 as a simple family tutoring project, but now delivers first-rate, free education primarily via their 2,000+ YouTube videos. The Los Gatos school system has used the Khan Academy to completely change the way classroom time is used. The students watch Khan Academy videos at their own pace in the classroom, and when they hit a stumbling block a teacher uses tools to identify the concept they are struggling with, and address that directly.[1]

I realize that there is validity to many of our assumptions about education; sometimes things are done a certain way because it's the best way to do them. Nobody wants random people teaching their children. That's fine, but you still need to go through the exercise to figure out whether you are accepting this because it's true or because it's less trouble than questioning it.

Killer Questions for Education

As we go through the rest of this chapter, I'm going to show you my stream of thought as I worked on creating my Killer Questions for education. This will give you a template that you can use for your own organization.

WHO

Growing up, I got a firsthand look at the ecosystem that surrounds education because my mom was on the local school board.

One time, my dad took me to a school board meeting so that I could experience a small, local version of democracy at work. I'll never forget the way that meeting degenerated into a shouting match (I don't recall over what), with adults resorting to calling each other names. There were many Whos in that meeting, all supposedly with the same goal, but at that moment, they seemed to want to kill one another. I recall looking around and noticing that I was the only student at the meeting.

As I drove home from my first meeting with the Department of Education, I thought about the people who had attended that meeting: teachers, principals, parents, and union reps. The one group not in attendance was students. However, the reality is that the education system is serving all of these Whos. They are all a part of the ecosystem and need to be considered. Therefore, the Who questions need to be written to accommodate all of them.

The *Who* questions I developed for the workshop were:

- What are the "buying" criteria used by parents when selecting how their children are educated? (e.g., an atmosphere with low incidence of school violence)
- What are the unshakable beliefs about what teachers want? (e.g., tenure)
- What unanticipated customer could benefit from education? (e.g., non-English-speaking parents taking ESL classes)

When you are rewriting the Killer Questions, avoid judgment words like *right, wrong, harms, fails, good,* and *bad.* The Killer Questions are written to focus on words that search for positive input (e.g., customer likes) and negative input (e.g., customer doesn't like), without suggesting what form the input might take. Look again at the third question: I specifically use words like "benefit" because they imply something of positive value without defining that value.

WHAT

When we started down the path of homeschooling our kids, we went about it the same way the school system does—namely, finding a set of grade-level curricula and teaching from them. The result was not so good.

What we discovered through the process of homeschooling was that there are three types of learners: visual, auditory, and tactile. And guess what—we got one of each. In addition, my wife and I discovered that we have different teaching styles. My wife's style is auditory/visual while my style was auditory/tactile. We realized that we needed to adjust our approach to homeschooling or else the results were going to be a disaster. So we created a custom curriculum for each child and tailored the teaching style to match. This is something that the school system is not set up to do. If one teacher is responsible for thirty kids, then only one-third of the kids in the classroom is being taught in a teaching style that matches their learning approach.

I wrote the following *What* questions for the workshop, keeping these personal experiences in mind as I did so:

- What groups find the public education system objectionable? (e.g., homeschool students, students who attend religious schools)
- What is surprisingly inefficient about the education process? (e.g., getting approval to experiment with new teaching methods)
- What skills will we need to teach students so they are competitive in the marketplace when they enter the job market? (e.g., critical-thinking skills applied to all subjects, entrepreneurship)

HOW

There is more to learning than what is taught in the classroom. Education needs to take a broader view of the value chain that can be leveraged to expand the knowledge and skills of our students. One group of participants in this value chain are organizations that will eventually hire graduates. So how do you include them? One idea is internships.

I'm a big believer in internships. They give us an opportunity to work with the best and the brightest beyond the act of hiring. I take the summer intern program to the extreme and select a few of the students to live with me during the summer. This extra step in the process of "manufacturing" a graduate ready to compete in the marketplace is mutually beneficial. The interns get all the mentoring they can handle, and I get three months with a new generation that would be hard to observe and understand otherwise.

So how do you go about looking at your *How* with that critical eye? There are multiple perspectives you can take when focusing on How. One is by viewing your value chain in terms of competitive pressures. I have the advantage of working in a highly competitive industry. I know the big players who are our direct competitors. I also know that there will always be someone and something new coming up that I can't predict or anticipate. The other option is to focus on efficiency. This approach relies on an organization's ability to look at each item in its value chain and attack it. If an item doesn't add value, then it gets dropped. For education, I went after efficiency.

The How questions I developed for the education workshop include:

- What are other educational approaches, and what can we learn from them? (e.g., apprenticeship)
- What do students *not* like about the classroom experience? (e.g, class time is boring)
- What do teachers *not* like about the classroom experience? (e.g., students aren't motivated to learn)

The "Innovate Education" Workshop

As soon as I decided to hold an innovation workshop on education, I invited my Twitter followers to sign up and participate. I limited the attendance to a dozen, and the event was at capacity within seventy-two hours. The event was on a Friday evening in San Jose, which, if you are familiar with Silicon Valley traffic patterns, is not a great time to attempt to get to an after-work event. Nonetheless, we had eleven people, including recent college graduates, the principal of an alternative school, two young entrepreneurs writing innovative education software, several parents, an innovator from Australia, and another attendee who traveled from New Orleans just to participate.

Everyone came with different objectives. Some wanted to attend a Killer Innovation workshop and apply their experience with the group to their own industry. Others merely had a desire to help improve education.

My objective for the workshop was to test the Killer Questions before handing them off to the Department of Education. Remember, the focus for the attendees of the workshop was *how to create innovations in education to better prepare our students for the competitive workforce.* I gave them the modified set of Killer Questions I'd written specifically for the project.

In order to make sure that all the questions were covered, I assigned the even-numbered questions to people with an even birth date (say, June 12). If their birth date was odd (say, August 25), they were assigned the odd-numbered questions.

I asked the participants to come up with at least fifteen observations for every question assigned. In the pre-workshop e-mail briefing, I reminded them that it is not about "solutions" (fixing the problem) at this stage. We would discuss possible solutions during the workshop. What I wanted them to do was to go out and challenge themselves and to go beyond the obvious. I told them the best thing to do was to get out and observe people as they experienced the education system. Sit down with their friends, their kids' friends, or teachers from their local schools. If they felt shy or awkward about this, I encouraged them to remember that most people love being asked for their opinion. Ask a few broad questions, and see where the conversation goes. Try not to steer the flow of your discussion, and let the participants cover the subjects that occur to them naturally. Once your interviewee feels comfortable, you can ask them the more challenging questions that they might have balked at out of the gate.

After a brief meet-and-greet, we sat down and started talking through the questions I'd assigned. The discussion quickly got very emotional and passionate as the attendees shared their observations.

I advised the group to use the same tips about generating ideas (break large ideas into smaller ones, try mixing and matching two ideas to make a third) that I discussed in chapter 9. Each person was invited to share their observations based on the questions they were assigned. Each item was written on a Post-it note and placed on a flip chart. When we were all done, there was a consensus emerging around the areas of biggest concern and their possible effects. Next, each person was tasked to come up with ideas, based on the questions, to address the focus of the workshop (creating innovations in education to better prepare our students for the competitive workforce). They were tasked to come up with twenty ideas in thirty minutes.

At the end of the half hour, we had literally hundreds of ideas, written out on color-coded Post-its for each individual. Some of the participants had used the strategies I discussed in the workshop chapter to turn one idea into two. For instance, one person came up with a first idea:

"Let's develop a curriculum that acknowledges the way students depend on their phones, and allows them to use them for voting or test-taking in the classroom."

Then he looked at the opposite of that first idea to make a second:

"Suppose we removed all technology from the schools and go 100 percent tech-free."

Each of these ideas has the potential to change the learning process, but in two radically different ways.

Once the ideas were introduced, they were then grouped to create themes of ideas.

The major groupings that emerged were:

- Teacher retirement based on a percentage of each students' eventual income.
- Reemphasize 4H, Boy Scouts, and Girl Scouts in the schools.
- Think global versus national or local about education.
- Stop focusing on best practices (copying what others do). It's about "next practice."
- Be willing to test alternative approaches to education.
- Make technology part of the education process.
- Teachers and students design curriculum.
- Corporate support for education.
- Rethink preparing students for post–high school when not going to college.
- Students teaching students.
- Work study/mentoring/apprenticeship to augment the classroom.
- Fix the "test-focused" approach to education.
- Look at the design of the classroom environment (lighting, work surfaces, etc.).
- Teach critical and creative-thinking skills across all subjects.
- Expand the use of specialty schools (magnet, science/technology, art, etc.).
- Bring back art, music, and foreign language.
- Re-create the teacher evaluation and pay system.
- Redesign the structure of the school day/year.
- Fix the funding model (e.g., change Prop 13 in California).
- Go digital—an education version of the electronic medical record (e.g., full transparency for parents).
- Change the homework (e.g., too much busywork rather than teaching).
- Dropout prevention.

- Administrator and teacher mentoring each other and doing a job rotation to avoid the us-versus-them mentality.
- Match teaching and learning styles (e.g., verbal, visual, tactile).

As with the Killer Questions, the ranking questions from the FIRE method were also rewritten to be appropriate to the education theme. As you should recall from chapter 9, the ranking questions are:

1. Does this idea change the customer experience or expectation?
2. Does this idea change your competitive positioning in the industry?
3. Does this idea change the economics of the industry?
4. Do you have a contribution to make?
5. Will this idea generate sufficient margin?

Remember: the first three questions focus on ranking the overall quality of the idea. The last two questions look at the ability to execute the idea, given the constraints and interests of the organization.

In this case, the objective was to create killer innovations for education to better prepare students for the highly competitive job market. Accordingly, the ranking questions I created were:

1. Will this idea change the **student's learning** experience/expectations?
2. Will this idea change the **competitiveness of the student**?
3. Will this idea improve the structure of the **education** industry?
4. Do we have **commitment to make this change**?

So, how would you rank the ideas listed above using the new ranking questions? If you want to see how the workshop ranked them, then visit my blog. Also, I hope that you consider this discussion about education an active exercise. If you'd like to participate, I'd love to hear your suggestions via my webpage or Twitter (or whatever tomorrow's version of Twitter turns out to be).

||||||||||||

As these case studies show, you can use the Killer Questions and the FIRE method to work on any kind of problem. I've had friends who've devised questions to figure out where their family should go on vacation. Their ranking questions look totally different from the traditional ones, but the process still works in the same way. Take this system and adapt it to suit your needs. Feel free to use the original set of questions as templates for the kind of questions you need.

Don't start by rewriting every question, though. Take a few at a time and see how you can refocus them for your individual needs or those of your organization. As you progress, try holding an informal workshop to test your questions and see what kinds of answers you get.

The Killer Questions are designed to evolve as industry, and the world in general, changes. I would love to hear examples of how you've radically taken apart or rewritten the Killer Questions, as well as how you've been able to make the kind of changes that have pushed your organization to the next level.

Go Forth and Innovate

B ack in 1995 or so, I noticed a sliver of an ad, one column wide and two lines deep, on the front page of the *New York Times*. I don't remember the exact wording, but the gist of it was "*Amazon .com, a river of books.*" I remember thinking that it must have been the cheapest ad the *Times* had ever sold on its cover, or perhaps it was an obscure prank. Instead, it was the opening shot in the war of old media versus new. I didn't know of Jeff Bezos then, and I wondered what buying this ad space meant to this unknown entrepreneur. Was it a massive gamble and leap of faith? Was he risking his family's financial future to buy that handful of words? Did he know where he was going and how he was going to get there?

I would love to go back in time and talk to Jeff about what he was thinking and feeling the moment he said, "OK, we're doing this," and placed that order for ad space. He and his partners were asking some pretty fundamental *How* Killer Questions about their customers' willingness to completely change the way they bought books, and there was no guarantee they were going to get the response they wanted. Recognizing the importance of asking the questions you'd never previously considered, and being willing to follow through on what you learn by asking them, is what separates those who succeed from those who fail. It can be scary—but the risks of inertia are worse.

As I've said throughout this book, I believe that the nature of the global economy is changing. If you want to be perceived as a highly valuable asset, either to your company or to your customers, you have to understand who you are, what you do, and how to change the way you work and generate value as well. What do you think your core value or skill is? If you are resting on an assumption that a deep-rooted and highly specialized knowledge or skill is enough to get you by, you are mistaken.

Knowledge used to be hard to acquire, and the difficulty of amassing it gave that knowledge—and the person who had it—value. A hundred years ago, there were very few avenues for an individual to learn how to do something. You could either apprentice, be born into a family business, or be rich and talented enough to be accepted into one of the very few universities. Part of the value of knowledge was its scarcity. This has changed, and it is going to continue to change as the information economy segues into the creative economy. The most valuable asset in this new economy is not simply technical ability or having a deeper level of knowledge than others in your field; it's your ability to apply your skills or knowledge in order to creatively come up with new ideas. It's no longer about what you can do with your hands but what you can come up with using your brain. If you can address the innovation gap for whatever organization you've aligned yourself with and present innovations that don't occur to your competitors, then you will have ensured the success of your organization.

It makes sense, really. The information that people have traditionally needed to succeed is becoming more and more accessible. When was the last time that Google was unable to answer a factual question for you? It's probably been a while. Remember the scene from *Catch Me If You Can,* where the antihero crams for the bar exam in one night, and passes, without having attended law school? That scene, whether fact or fiction, is a good metaphor for how the nature of information as a product is continuing to change. He got his hands on the relevant books, applied himself to the task, and took the test. His knowledge may have been superficial, and he probably wouldn't have lasted one day in court, but he was able to absorb enough information to pass the bar and get his foot in the door. And that was fifty years ago, long before the Internet age.

These days, anybody with ambition, a sense of curiosity, and access to the web can learn what used to be restricted to the elite and the lucky. The explosive growth of the university systems in India and China are creating a vast population of people who *have the same specialized knowledge as you do*. In many cases, these armies of graduates are willing to sell that knowledge for substantially less than you are. As a result, your knowledge will no longer guarantee you a career. The people in charge no longer need you to have all the answers. They need you be able to ask the questions that lead to the right innovations.

By reading *Beyond the Obvious*, you are starting down the path to becoming a key player in the creative economy. But reading alone isn't enough. You've learned the basics, but now you have to practice and apply these skills to real-world scenarios. And the more you apply them, the more you practice them, and the more you adapt them, the more you'll find what works for you and the better you will be at asking the right questions. The key is to build up the confidence in yourself that you can take this leap, especially if you've never considered yourself a "creative" talent. Creativity is not a gift from God, and if you insist on seeing it that way, you're simply giving yourself an excuse not to try.

Still, some people don't believe that they can generate the ideas their companies need. A story from a few years ago, when a client of mine acquired a small start-up, illustrates the reasoning behind this mindset perfectly. As part of the process of introducing the new team, they hosted a session and invited employees to come and learn about the products and the people who would be joining their organization. They had a hundred or so people in the room, and the session quickly turned into an impromptu workshop about innovation, the nature of ideas, and ways that ideas could be generated. I got pretty energized and pumped; the conversation was going back and forth; and the group was full of ideas about how to leverage the new acquisition's products and technologies. I love this kind of animated and excited mix. They brought prototypes in and showed the new team what some of tomorrow's products were going to look like. They were thrilled, because this rarely happens. Most people are incredibly secretive with new products because they're worried about leaks.

At the end of the session, I asked the people in the room a rhetorical question: "What is preventing any of you from being able to walk out of this room and become the innovation evangelist?" After all, I don't speak at these events just to hear myself talk or to have a group come up afterward and tell me how great the speech was. My whole purpose is to equip others to be innovation spokespeople within their own department, industry, or organization, not only in terms of letting their coworkers or contemporaries know what's "coming next," but also in demonstrating how to apply it when it does. I want people to walk out feeling they have the ability to be innovative within their own team, whatever their role is.

I felt pretty good about this group. Everyone seemed to understand the message, and they showed enthusiasm about taking the ideas I presented about innovation, and the Killer Questions, and doing something with them. As I was wrapping up the session, I noticed a hand pop up. I pointed to the person and asked what his question was. He said, "Phil, great session. However, I don't think I can be innovative back in my organization." I replied, "What do you mean?" He said, "Well, my manager hasn't given me permission to innovate."

I think time literally stood still for a second. I'd just finished a discussion that was focused on telling a whole bunch of people that they all have an inner spark of creativity that they can and *must* embrace. I didn't understand how one person could allow another person to tell him that he was *not allowed to come up with new ideas*. It seriously didn't make sense. Even if innovation isn't part of your job description, your mind, your ingenuity, and your ambition are your own. No one can tell you not to use them. We are all free to look at a problem or opportunity, ask questions, think about what we see, and come up with solutions or ideas to address it. Still somewhat dumbfounded, I asked him, "Are you seriously waiting for someone from senior management to come down to your cubicle and give you permission to innovate? Here, I'm going to solve this problem really fast for everybody in the room." I put my hands up in the air and said, in my best Moses voice, "I hereby grant you all permission to innovate. Now, any questions?"

I truly hope that my "permission to innovate," no matter how humorous it may have seemed at the time, stirred something in all of the attendees. Because that's what I believe; you can't wait for someone to tell you that it's OK to try. It's up to *you* to take that first step. When it comes to innovation and ideas, nobody has ownership or control over you. Nobody can tell you that "*coming up with new ideas isn't part of your job description.*" Nobody can stop you from being creative, unless you are willing to let them stop you.

I understand that some organizations and business cultures can be very controlling. It's possible that you wake up in the morning with the energy and the enthusiasm to focus on the tiniest germ of an idea that you think has potential. But then you get to work and your boss says, "I need you to do these five things for me today." And then tomorrow you come in, and your boss says, "I need you to do these four things for me today." Despite all your energy, you can't escape that you have a very task-oriented employer, instead of one who might say something like *Hey, if you see a problem, or something just isn't working right and you think you've got a better way of doing it, then figure out a way to go do it your way.* I'm going to give you the same piece of advice I mentioned in chapter 3 when talking about corporate antibodies: Sometimes you have to take a chance. If you have a great idea and you truly believe in it, then push. And keep pushing. If you asked the Killer Questions, and followed the FIRE method, then you have a good idea. Have faith in it, have faith in yourself. If you can't get traction for your idea at your current organization, consider what other alternatives are open to you. Perhaps your idea is worth taking a personal risk on, or perhaps you need to find an organization willing to support what you do.

There is no magic to this stuff. I've been able to succeed because I've generated a system that guides me past the obvious ideas and straight toward the breakthrough idea. I also have the confidence to push for my ideas and make sure they get a chance to prove themselves. So, if you find yourself with a great idea but are lacking the will or the ability to push it through, be aware that the weakest link in the chain isn't your idea, but your belief in yourself. Start small and build up. Present an idea that's modest in ambition, and get used to the feeling of putting yourself in the spotlight and having to push for your ideas. When that works, come back with a bigger idea, and so on. Remember that confidence can be learned. If you don't have it now, give yourself the chance to gain it with small victories.

As I've mentioned throughout this book, innovation is a skill that anybody can learn. But it's also like playing a sport: If you want to play golf and you want to get really good at it, then you've got to go out and practice. You have to go to the driving range. You have to hit balls.

So, what happens if you have a few misfires? Keep trying; don't let early mistakes scare you out of making another attempt. Remember, you can have a great idea that doesn't work because of poor timing. However, you need to have the fortitude to keep going, even after working on something that doesn't come to fruition. One thing I've noticed from my dealings with businesses and entrepreneurs around the world is how we can benefit from refusing to attach any stigma to ideas that previously didn't pan out. Within forward-looking organizations, an idea can miss the mark and still get another chance.

Right now, Silicon Valley is in the middle of a hiring boom. Google, Facebook, Twitter, and a great number of other companies are searching for the best talent to fuel their growth. Venture capitalists are taking risks and investing with energetic start-ups that have some great ideas. It's as though the setbacks of the late '90s and late 2000s had never happened. And that's a fantastic thing. You always get a second chance in the changing landscape of ideas, no matter how badly you may have failed in the past.

||||||||||||

If you've read this book and it hasn't changed you, then I've failed in writing it. *Beyond the Obvious* is about changing how people view themselves, and what they're capable of. It's about giving them the confidence to ignore the path everyone else is on and think differently about their own ability to be innovative.

It is still disheartening and rather amazing to think that so many people believe that this "creative ability" is reserved for a subset of people within their organization. "Oh, I'm just the receptionist," one might say. Well, suppose that receptionist comes up with a seemingly simple way to streamline some routine office procedure, such as filing expense reports? Over a few years, that could have a huge effect on the organization. And if you think that there's no one out there supporting you or believing in you, then you're mistaken. Just by virtue of the fact that you are buying and using this book, I am invested in your work. Drop me a line at feedback@philmckinney.com and let me know how you're doing.

It doesn't matter what your role is. It doesn't matter what your education level is. It doesn't matter where you live in the world. The purpose of this book is for you to take your ideas and apply them to whatever it is that you're passionate about, perhaps within your business, the nonprofit you volunteer at, or your personal career. You can make change happen, and you can generate the ideas that spark revolutions in how we do things, be it on a personal level or a global one.

Now is the time to put down the book, open the door, and *go forth and innovate*.

Follow the author's blog and podcast at:
philmckinney.com

*For additional content and updates, and to join in the
conversation with other readers of the book, visit:*
BeyondTheObvious.com

Acknowledgments

Many have the perception that writing a book is the output of one person's solitary effort, but that is not the case. This book came into existence from experiences, conversations, projects, and support from a number of people. I can't begin to acknowledge all of them, and if I leave you off the list, chalk it up to my forgetfulness and not any attempt to slight anyone.

First, to God be the glory. For His unconditional love and for giving me more than one person deserves. Everything I have comes from Him. For the men God put in my path to ensure I didn't go off track—Mike Kiley and Gary Grogan.

The core of this book is the result of key events in my life. The first was being recruited into my first job by Bob Davis, who started me down this crazy path of "feeding my curiosity." The result was that I stumbled upon a mentor whose impact on my career I can never pay back.

Another was the break I took in my career after my stint at Teligent. During that short "retirement," I finally slowed down enough to put to paper my experiences and lessons learned, which eventually became the core of this book. A number of people played a key role in the early refinement of the ideas, including: Alex and Susan Mandl, Mark Varricchione, Mike Stutz, David Chew, Abe Morris, D. P. Venkatesh, Michael Keeler, Samer Omar, and Adi Gan.

Then came the Killer Innovations podcast. What started out as an experiment to see if anyone was interested quickly turned into a community. The list of listeners, followers, and supporters is far too long for me to include everybody, but each and every one of them deserves to be listed. It was their feedback, suggestions, stories, and even criticism that provided the fuel to keep working and refining the ideas.

I'm a believer in success from teamwork, and the success I've had is directly attributable to the innovation teams that I've had the privilege to lead. Their feedback and support was invaluable. Members have included: Mamoun Abu-Samaha, Patti Ballard, Steve Balsiger, Harry Beane, Gene Becker, Jim Bell, Masumi Blair, Andrew Bolwell, Curtis Brown, Mark Budgell, Mickie Calkins, Paul Campbell, Ozzie Diaz, Luca Di Fiore, Eleanore Dogan, Jeff Edlund, Ann Finnie, Darren Gladstone, Nick Hallas, Jean Ibanez, Valerie Ko, Deepa Kumar, Tom Matthews, Paul Martin, Doug McMahon, Robert Mihalik, Carlos Montalvo, Cornelia Oehler, Bea Onsurez, Carol Ozaki, Christian Pape, Allen Proithis, Amy Reardon, Diana Robbins, Soma Santhiveeran, David R. Smith, Marlene Somsak, Mark Solomon, Rahul Sood, Ravi Sood, Hari Subraminam, Sankar Sundaresan, Qi-Bin Sun, Tom Szolyga, Michael Takemura, James Taylor, Jim Vanides, Peter Vesterbacka, Susie Wee, Tony Welch, and Glen Wong.

To the HP Labs team, who is tasked to "invent the future." Without their energy, passion, and ideas, the innovation funnel wouldn't have been nearly as much fun or had as much of an impact. Of special note is the support I received from Dick Lampman, Prith Banerjee, John Sontag, Henry Sang, Nelson Chang, John Apostolopoulos, April Slayden-Mitchell, Alex Vorbau, Patrick Goddi, Rajan Lukose, Jaap Suermondt, Kar Han Tan, Mitch Trott, Bowon Lee, Harlyn Baker, and Rich Friedrich.

As with any effort, innovation stands on the shoulders of others, and it is no different with this effort. There are many who have gone before me who have influenced my thinking, including: Bill Hewlett, David Packard, Art Fong, Chuck House, Shane Robison, John Cochran, Wendell Weeks, Waguih Ishak, John Riccitiello, Joe Pine, Geoffrey Moore, Jeffrey Katzenberg, Ed Leonard, Michael Mendenhall, Satjiv Chahill, John Osborne, Brett Bonner, Steve Hellmuth, Andy Schwalb, Mark Henderson, Abdul Bengali, Len Sherman, Richard Edelman, Jeff Mirich, Robert Sauerberg, Joe Simon, Matthias Essen-preis, Sebastiaan la Bastide, Radiris Diaz, Michael Reyes, John Obeto, Vince Pace, Jimmy Iovine, and will.i.am.

When you write a book, there is an entire team behind you that assists in bringing all of the pieces together. This includes my literary agent, Marc Gerald, who helped a novice navigate the process of going from a nugget of an idea to a finished book, and his team, Sasha Raskin and Molly Derse, who went beyond the call of duty in supporting me throughout the project.

One very special person I need to thank is Caroline Greeven. Caroline took on the task of going through the content from the podcasts, speeches, and blog posts, and then helped me organize, structure, and pull it all together into this book. I can't thank her enough for the time, patience, and skill she brought to this project.

All of this would not be possible without the Hyperion team, including Elisabeth Dyssegaard, editor-in-chief at Hyperion, who recognized the value of bringing the ideas out in a book; and the person who ensured that it all made sense in the end, Matt Inman, my editor.

That brings me to the support and encouragement of those people without whom this book would not have happened, my family. My children, Oliver, Tara, Brian, Rachel, and Logan, who continually renew my hope for the future. I'm so proud of them. At the very center of everything is my wife, Michelle. Writing is a journey that takes you away from your loved ones. Through evenings, weekends, and forfeited vacations, Michelle was there to take on the tasks that would normally fall on my shoulders and to be an encouragement through the whole process. Without her support and constant prayer, I would have nothing to give to others.

Notes

Introduction

1   Slate, John. "Southwestern Telegraph & Telephone Company."
    Dallas Municipal Archives. 10 June 2005. http://www.ci.dallas
    .tx.us/cso/archives/FindingGuides/91-026w.pdf
2   Telecommunications Act of 1996. FCC. 15 November 2008.
    http://transition.fcc.gov/telecom.html
3   "AT&T Making a Move." The Associated Press. *New York
    Times*. 30 June 2008. http://www.nytimes.com/2008/06/30/
    technology/30phone.html
4   Balmoris, Mike. "FCC Approves SBC-Ameritech Merger Subject
    to Competition-Enhancing Conditions." *FCC News*. 6 October
    1999. http://transition.fcc.gov/Bureaus/Common_Carrier/News_
    Releases/1999/nrcc9077.html; Vorman, Julie. "AT&T Closes
    $86 Billion SouthBell Deal." Reuters. 29 December 2006. http://
    www.reuters.com/article/2007/01/02/businesspro-bellsouth-fcc
    -dc-idUSWBT00636120070102
5   "Offering Customers a New Leader in Entertainment." AT&T
    Newsroom. 18 November 2005. http://www.att.com/gen/press
    -room?pid=4800&cdvn=news&newsarticleid=21906

6   "The Apollo 13 Accident." NASA. 19 November 2009. http://
nssdc.gsfc.nasa.gov/planetary/lunar/ap13acc.html

7   2010 Annual Report. Investor Relations. HP. http://h30261
.www3.hp.com/phoenix.zhtml?c=71087&p=irol-irhome

8   Roos, Gina. "HP, Dell Ranked as Top Global PC Makers." *Electronics Advocate*. 6 September 2010. http://www.electronics
advocate.com/2010/09/06/hp-dell-ranked-as-top-global-pc-makers/

Chapter 1: Why Questions Matter

1   Pierre-Marc-Gaston, duc de Lévis. *Maximes et réflexions sur différents sujets de morale et de politique* (Paris, 1808): Maxim xvii.

2   Jordania, Joseph. "Who Asked the First Question?" International Research Centre of Traditional Polyphony, 2006. http://
www.polyphony.ge/uploads/whoaskthefirst.pdf

3   Zimmer, Carl. "From Ants to People, an Instinct to Swarm."
New York Times, 13 November 2007. http://www.nytimes.com
/2007/11/13/science/13traff.html?pagewanted=all

4   Franks, Nigel R. "Army Ants: A Collective Intelligence."
American Scientist, 77:139, 1989.

5   Carson, Shelley. "The Unleashed Mind: Why Creative People Are Eccentric." *Scientific American,* 14 April 2011. http://www
.scientificamerican.com/article.cfm?id=the-unleashed-mind

6   "Leading Question." Legal Information Institute. Cornell University Law School. 19 August 2010. http://topics.law.cornell
.edu/wex/leading_question

7   "The Socratic Method." Thomas Aquinas College, 2011. http://
www.thomasaquinas.edu/curriculum/socratic.htm

Chapter 2: Questioning Your Assumptions, Managing Your Jolts

1   "Milacron History." Milacron. http://www.milacron.com/co/
about/milhistory.htm

2   Wieandt, Axel. "Innovation and the Creation, Development and Destruction of Markets in the World Machine Tool Industry."
Small Business Economics, December 1994.

3   "Joint UNOVA and Cincinnati Milacron News Release: UNOVA
     to Buy Cincinnati Milacron's Machine Tool Group for $178
     Million in Cash." *Business Wire*, 21 August 1998.

4   Lewin, Tamar. "Tylenol Maker Finding New Crisis Less Severe."
     New York Times, 12 February 1986. http://www.nytimes.com
     /1986/02/12/business/tylenol-maker-finding-new-crisis-less
     -severe.html

5   "How Google Works." *The Economist*, 16 September 2004.

6   Wilson, Dean. "Google Wanted to Sell Its Soul for One Million
     Dollars." *Techeye*, 30 September 2010. http://www.techeye.net/
     business/google-wanted-to-sell-its-soul-for-1-million

7   "In a Death Seen Around the World, a Symbol of Iranian
     Protests." *New York Times*, 22 June 2009. http://www.nytimes
     .com/2009/06/23/world/middleeast/23neda.html?ref=middleeast

8   "Pilot landed in Hudson to avoid 'catastrophic consequences.'"
     CNN, 18 February2009. http://www.cnn.com/2009/US/01/17
     /hudson.plane.crash/index.html#cnnSTCText

Chapter 3: The Corporate Antibodies

1   Anders, George. "Behind the Screen at Hewlett-Packard."
     Forbes, 22 October 2009. http://www.forbes.com/2009/10/21/
     hewlett-packard-hp-phenomenon-opinions-contributors-book
     -review-george-anders.html

2   Packard, David. *The HP Way*. New York: HarperCollins, 2006.

3   Malone, Michael Shawn. *Bill & Dave: How Hewlett and Packard
     Built the World's Greatest Company*. New York: Penguin, 2007,
     p. 225.

4   "Apollo: Humankind's First Steps on the Lunar Surface."
     NASA, 8 July 2009. http://www.nasa.gov/mission_pages/apollo/
     apollo11_40th.html

5   Henkel, John. "Attacking AIDS with a 'Cocktail' Therapy." *FDA
     Consumer*, July 1999.

6   "For Tom Ford Runway Shows Aimed at Critics Are Out as He
     Focuses on the Customer." *CrashCollective*, 21 February 2011.

http://crashcollective.com/uncategorized/for-tom-ford-runway
-shows-aimed-at-critics-are-out-as-he-focuses-on-the-customer/

7   Cartner-Morley, Jess. "Tom Ford Rewrites Rulebook in Surprise
New York Comeback." *The Guardian,* 13 September 2010.
http://www.guardian.co.uk/lifeandstyle/2010/sep/13/tom-ford
-surprise-new-york-comeback

8   Menkes, Suzy. "A Heroic Return to Fashion." *New York Times,*
13 September 2010. http://www.nytimes.com/2010/09/14/
fashion/14iht-rford.html

9   Wozniak, Steve. *iWoz: From Computer Geek to Cult Icon: How
I Invented the Personal Computer, Co-Founded Apple, and Had
Fun Doing It.* W.W. Norton, 2006.

10 "Wozniak Tells His Side of the Story." *Sydney Morning Herald,*
September 2006. http://www.smh.com.au/news/laptops
–desktops/wozniak-tells-his-side-of-the-story/2006/09/28/
1159337270259.html; "A Chat with Computing Pioneer Steve
Wozniak." NPR, 29 September 2006. http://www.npr.org/
templates/story/story.php?storyId=6167297

Chapter 5: The FIRE Method

1   "Gordian Systems." PhilMcKinney.com, http://philmckinney.com/
portfolio/Gordian_Systems.pdf

2   "Thumbscan." PhilMcKinney.com, http://philmckinney.com/
portfolio/ThumbScan.pdf

3   Glancey, Jonathan. "What Has Labour Done for Architecture?"
The Guardian, 21 April 2010. http://www.guardian.co.uk/
artanddesign/2010/apr/21/labour-party-architecture

4   "Dome Woes Haunt Blair." BBC News, 15 February 2001.
http://news.bbc.co.uk/2/hi/uk_news/politics/1172367.stm

5   "UK Politics." BBC News, 24 December 1998. http://news.bbc
.co.uk/2/hi/uk_news/politics/241684.stm

6   Reed, Lawrence. "A Lesson from Great Britain." Mackinac
Center for Public Policy, 3 February, 2003. http://www.mackinac
.org/4999

7   Page, Jennifer. "My Crown of Thorns." *The Guardian,* 4 May 2000. http://www.guardian.co.uk/uk/2000/may/04/dome .millennium1

8   "Reopening an Old Wound." The Economist, 21 June 2007. http://www.economist.com/node/9370629

Chapter 6: Getting to Know Your *Who*

1   "HP Connects Consumers in India to World Wide Web, Hometown Content." HP.com. http://www.hp.com/hpinfo/newsroom/ press/2010/101118b.html

2   Dybwad, Barb. "Microsoft Announces the HP Touchsmart PC." *Engadget,* 1 January 2007. http://www.engadget.com/2007/01/ 07/microsoft-announces-the-hp-touchsmart-pc/; "HP Unveils New Multitouch PCs and Display." HP.com, 13 October 2009. http://www.hp.com/hpinfo/newsroom/press/2009/091013xc.html

3   McKinney, Phil. 2009 January 9. *How HP Innovates.* Consumer Electronics Show. Las Vegas, NV.

4   Mills, Jeff. "Airbus A380 vs. Boeing Dreamliner." *The Telegraph,* 2 February 2008. http://www.telegraph.co.uk/travel/737906/ Airbus-A380-vs-Boeing-Dreamliner.html

5   Rothwell, Steve, and Andrea Rothman. "Airbus's a380 Bypasses Hubs to Target Smaller Cities." *BusinessWeek.* 8 October 2010. http://www.businessweek.com/news/2010-10-08/airbus-s-a380 -bypasses-hubs-to-target-smaller-cities.html

6   Goodell, Andrea. "Crafty Calling." *The Holland Sentinel,* 14 December 2010. http://www.hollandsentinel.com/feature/ x1714281737/Crafty-Calling-More-than-50-Holland-artisans -ride-trend-of-homemade-wares

7   Linkins, Jason. "Urban Outfitters Continues Their Tradition of Ripping Off Designers." *Huffington Post,* 26 May 2011. http:// www.huffingtonpost.com/2011/05/26/urban-outfitters-steal_n_ 867604.html

8   Wachman, Richard. "Dutch Bankers' Bonuses Axed by People Power." *The Guardian,* 27 March 2011. http://www.guardian.co

.uk/business/2011/mar/27/dutch-bankers-bonuses-axed-by
-people-power

9   "Virgin: The World's Best Passenger Complaint Letter." *The Tele-graph*, 26 January 2009. http://www.telegraph.co.uk/travel/
travelnews/4344890/Virgin-the-worlds-best-passenger-complaint
-letter.html

10   "United Airlines Gives to Charity in Guitar Gaffe." *The Star*
(Canada), July 2009. http://www.thestar.com/news/canada/
article/664557

11   Hormby, Tom. "The Story Behind Apple's Newton." 7 February
2006. http://lowendmac.com/orchard/06/john-sculley-newton
-origin.html

12   Robbins, William. "Teflon Maker: Out of Frying Pan into
Fame." *New York Times,* 21 December 1986. Section 1, p. 26.
http://www.nytimes.com/1986/12/21/us/teflon-maker-out-of
-frying-pan-into-fame.html

13   "Inventor of the Week. Art Fry and Spencer Silver." MIT.edu.
http://web.mit.edu/invent/iow/frysilver.html

14   "Frequency Divider Extends Automatic Digital Frequency
Measurements to 12.4 GHz." *HP Journal*, April 1967. http://
www.hpl.hp.com/hpjournal/pdfs/IssuePDFs/1967-04.pdf; "The
Linear Quartz Thermometer." *HP Journal,* March 1965. http://
www.hpl.hp.com/hpjournal/pdfs/IssuePDFs/1965-03.pdf

15   McCracken, Harry. "20 Years of AOL Annoyances and Foul-ups." *PC World,* April 2009. http://www.pcworld.com/article/
163935/20_years_of_aol_annoyances_and_foulups.html

Chapter 7: What Is Your *What?*

1   Trademark of Individual Software, Inc.

2   LaPlante, Alice. "Benefits of OS/2 Similar to the Mac's, IBM Says."
Info World, January 1988, pp. 1–85; Quinlan, Tom. "Apple Finally
Says It Will License Mac OS." *Info World,* January 1994, pp. 1–99.

3   "Wang Resculpts Its Image." *Network World,* August 1987.

4   "Emirates Replaces United Airlines as World's Largest Carrier."

Centre for Aviation, 2 March 2011. http://www.centreforaviation
.com/news/2011/03/02/emirates-replaces-united-airlines-as
-worlds-third-largest-carrier-top-25-rankings/page1

5   Flottau, Jens, and Max Kingsley-Jones. "Defensive Posture."
    Aviation Week & Space Technology, 11 November 2010.

6   "Who's Where?" *Aviation Week & Space Technology*, December
    2010, p. 10.

7   Epstein, Edward. "Have You Ever Tried to Sell a Diamond?" *The
    Atlantic,* February 1982. http://www.theatlantic.com/magazine
    /archive/1982/02/have-you-ever-tried-to-sell-a-diamond/4575/

8   Roberts, Janine. "Masters of Illusion." *The Ecologist,* 1 September
    2003. http://www.theecologist.org/investigations/politics_and_
    economics/268557/masters_of_illusion.html

9   Schooley, Tim. "Does De Beers Ad Campaign Ring True?"
    Pittsburgh Business Times, 1 March 2004. http://www.bizjournals
    .com/pittsburgh/stories/2004/03/01/focus2.html

10 Pine, J., and J. Gilmore. *The Experience Economy.* Boston:
    Harvard Business School Press, 1999.

11 "Condé Naste Traveller iPhone City Guides." CNTraveller.com.
    http://www.cntraveller.com/iphone/

12 Foiret, Cyril. "Interview Magazine First Mag for iPad." Trend-
    land, 1 April 2010. http://trendland.net/2010/04/01/interview
    -magazine-first-mag-for-ipad/

13 "HP's nod to women in IT." IT Sneak. 26 March 2009. http://
    www.v3.co.uk/v3-uk/it-sneak-blog/2020671/hps-nod-women-it.

14 McKinney, Phil. 2009 January 9. *How HP Innovates.* Consumer
    Electronics Show. Las Vegas, NV.

15 "Amazon's A9 Search as We Knew It: Dead!" *PCWorld,* September
    2006. http://blogs.pcworld.com/techlog/archives/002876.html

16 Amazon Web Services: Amazon S3. http://aws.typepad.com/aws/
    2008/10/amazon-s3—now.html

17 "The *Sputnik* Program." NOVA Online, February 2010. http://
    novaonline.nvcc.edu/eli/evans/his135/Events/Sputnik57/back
    ground.html

Chapter 8: How It Gets Done

1   "Billion Dollar Bonanza." ComScore.com, 1 December 2010.
    http://www.comscore.com/Press_Events/Press_Releases/2010/12/
    Billion_Dollar_Bonanza_Cyber_Monday_Surpasses_1_Billion_
    in_U.S._Spending

2   Wray, Richard. "Boo.com Spent Fast and Died Young but Its
    Legacy Shaped Internet Retailing." *The Guardian,* 16 May 2005.
    http://www.guardian.co.uk/technology/2005/may/16/media
    .business

3   Ward, Marc. "From Boo.com to Boo.gone." *BBC News,* 18 May
    2000. http://news.bbc.co.uk/2/hi/business/753782.stm

4   Dobbin, Ben. "If Only Kodak Had Phased Out Celluloid
    Sooner." *USA Today,* 8 September 2005. http://www.usatoday
    .com/tech/news/2005-09-08-kodak-digital-camera_x.htm; "We
    Had No Idea." *Plugged In,* October 2007. http://pluggedin
    .kodak.com/pluggedin/post/?id=687843

5   Christensen, Clayton. *The Innovator's Dilemma.* Boston:
    Harvard Business School Press, 1997.

6   Vance, Ashlee. "HP Labs Pulls Out the Measuring Stick." *New
    York Times,* 29 April 2009. http://bits.blogs.nytimes.com/2009/04/
    29/hp-labs-pulls-out-the-measuring-stick/; "HP and Strategic
    Management Solutions." Cornell School of Operations Research
    and Information Engineering, April 2010. http://www.orie.cornell
    .edu/news/news/profile3.cfm?customel_dataPageID_3742=153973

7   Leland, John. "A Church that Packs Them In, 16,000 at a Time."
    New York Times, 18 July 2005. http://www.nytimes.com/2005/
    07/18/national/18lakewood.html

8   "Demand Dinged." *Aviation Week & Space Technology,* 11 April
    2011, p. 40; "For Delta, Japan Remains Key." *Aviation Week &
    Space Technology,* 28 March 2011, p. 13.

9   "Shin-Etsu's Shirakawa Plant Returning to Pre-Quake Wafer
    Operation by July." Semiconportal: EmergingTech from Japan, 2
    May 2011. https://www.semiconportal.com/en/archive/news/
    main-news/110502-shin-etsu-wafer-shirakawa-resumption.html;

Miyoung Kim and Clare Jim. "Asian Supply Chain Rattled by Japan Quake Tsunami." *International Business Times,* 14 March 2011. http://www.ibtimes.com/articles/122170/20110314/asian -supply-chain-rattled-by-japan-quake-tsunami.htm

10 "History of the 9100A Desktop Calculator, 1968." HP.com. http://www.hp.com/hpinfo/abouthp/histnfacts/museum/personal systems/0021/0021history.html

11 "HP Timeline—1960s." HP.com. http://www.hp.com/hpinfo/ abouthp/histnfacts/timeline/hist_60s.html

12 Smith, Robert. "Eames Lounge Chair Exhibition at the Museum of Arts and Design." *New York Times,* 26 May 2006. http:// www.nytimes.com/2006/05/26/arts/design/26eame.html?_r=1

13 "Reaching the Next Billion." HP.com. http://www.hp.com/ hpinfo/globalcitizenship/global_issues/reaching_the_next_billion .html

14 "An Analysis of Small Business Patents by Industry and Firm Size." Small Business Administration (SBA), November 2008. http://archive.sba.gov/advo/research/rs335tot.pdf

15 "The World's Most Innovative Companies." *BusinessWeek,* 24 April 2006. http://www.businessweek.com/magazine/content/06_ 17/b3981401.htm

16 Veila, Matt, and Reena Jana. "Ford's Green Plan to Drive Sales." *BusinessWeek,* 8 December 2008. http://www.businessweek.com/ innovate/content/dec2008/id2008128_787972.htm

17 O'Connor, Ashling. "Tata Nano." *The Sunday Times,* 11 January 2008. http://www.timesonline.co.uk/tol/driving/article3164205 .ece

18 "2011 Tata Nano U.S. Intro Expected." *The Auto Writer,* 8 June 2009. http://thearticlewriter.com/autowriter/2011-tata-nano-us -intro-expected/

19 "The (Virtual) Doctor Will See You Now." *Fast Company,* May 2011.

20 Krieger, Todd. "Love and Money." *Wired.* September 1995. http://www.wired.com/wired/archive/3.09/scans.html?pg=7r

21 Lee, Amy. "Match.com Buys OKCupid Site." *Huffington Post*. 2 February 2011. http://www.huffingtonpost.com/2011/02/02/ matchcom-buys-okcupid_n_817368.html

22 "The FedEx Express SuperHub in Memphis." FedEx.com. http://news.van.fedex.com/files/FedEx%20Express%20Super% 20Hub%20in%20Memphis.pdf

23 Valdes-Dapena, Peter. "Saturn: Secrets of the No Haggle Price." CNN, 19 September 2006. http://money.cnn.com/2006/09/19/ autos/debating_no-haggle/index.htm

24 Holt, Brady. "What Happened to Saturn, and What's Happening Now?" *The Examiner*, 24 February 2009. http://www.examiner .com/autos-in-national/what-happened-to-saturn-and-what-s -happening-now-general-motors-asks-for-patience

25 Beale, Stephen. "More on Apple's Sales Figures." *Macworld*, 27 January 2001. http://www.macworld.com/article/21880/2001/01/ numbers.html

26 "The Stores." IfoAppleStore.com. http://www.ifoapplestore.com/ the_stores.html

27 "Yearly & Quarterly Financial Results." IfoAppleStore.com. http://www.ifoapplestore.com/stores/charts_graphs.html

28 Peterson, Peter. "Will America Grow Up Before It Grows Old?" *The Atlantic*. May 1996. http://www.theatlantic.com/past/docs/ issues/96may/aging/aging.htm

Chapter 9: Working the Workshop

1 Kawasaki, Guy. "The 10/20/30 Rule of PowerPoint." *How to Change the World*, 30 December 2005. http://blog.guykawasaki .com/2005/12/the_102030_rule.html#axzz1OAzPWYRX

Chapter 10: Adopt and Adapt

1 Whittemore, Nathaniel. "Big Ideas from TED 2011: Letting Students Drive Their Education." *Good Education*, March 2011. http://www.good.is/post/big-ideas-from-ted-2011-letting-students -drive-their-education

Index